1001

TOUGHEST
TV
TRIVIA
QUESTIONS
OF ALL TIME

Vincent Terrace

A CITADEL PRESS BOOK
Published by Carol Publishing Group

A Citadel Press Book
Published by Carol Publishing Group
Citadel Press is a registered trademark of Carol Communications, Inc.
Editorial Offices: 600 Madison Avenue, New York, N.Y. 10022
Sales and Distribution Offices: 120 Enterprise Avenue, Secaucus, N.J. 07094
In Canada: Canadian Manda Group, P.O. Box 920, Station U, Toronto, Ontario   M8Z 5P9
Queries regarding rights and permissions should be addressed to Carol Publishing Group, 600 Madison Avenue, New York, N.Y. 10022

Carol Publishing Group books are available at special discounts for bulk purchases, for sales promotion, fund-raising, or educational purposes. Special editions can be created to specifications. For details, contact: Special Sales Department, Carol Publishing Group, 120 Enterprise Avenue, Secaucus, N.J. 07094

Manufactured in the United States of America
10 9 8 7 6 5 4 3 2 1

Library of Congress Cataloging-in-Publication Data

Terrace, Vincent, 1948–
    1001 toughest TV trivia questions of all time / Vincent Terrace.
        p.   cm.
    "A Citadel Press book."
    ISBN 0-8065-1499-X (pbk.)
    1. Television programs—United States—Miscellaneous. I. Title.
PN1992.9.T46   1994
791.45′75′0973—dc20
                                                             93-47397
                                                                 CIP

CONTENTS

iii

Chapter 2: Drama and Adventure   159

Chapter 3: Kid Shows, Science Fiction Series and Westerns   229

INTRODUCTION

TELEVISION EXPERTS TAKE NOTICE. This is not your typical question-and-answer book. It is a butt buster. Sure, you may know that the Munsters lived at 1313 Mockingbird Lane and that Fred and Wilma Flintstone resided in the town of Bedrock. But do you know what Herman Munster's blood pressure was? Or what type of pet Fred and Wilma had? If you do, then this book is right up your alley. If not, you'll be provided with an education in TV trivia that you can't find anyplace else.

No, you won't find questions like "What is the color of 'The Green Hornet's black car" or "On what network does the 'ABC Afterschool Special' air?" You'll find narratives that first provide information on a show, then ask you a question about that show. In a number of cases, the characters to which the question refers provide their own answers.

As you peruse the book you'll notice that the 237 series listed here are ones you heard of and saw and in most cases, remember. Obscure programs and shows are not used here to compile questions. What fun is trying to answer a question on a program you never even heard of? To make for a more interesting book, several questions were used per show rather than using 1001 questions from as many different shows, to give you a better chance of answering a number of questions correctly.

So, sit back, put that thinking cap on, and take the challenge by answering *1001 Toughest TV Trivia Questions of All Time.*

HOW TO USE
1001 Toughest TV Trivia Questions of All Time

THIS BOOK is divided into three sections: Comedy; Drama and Adventure; and Kid Shows, Science Fiction Series and Westerns. Each section contains questions and answers pertaining to particular shows. Within each section, shows are listed in alphabetical order.

For your convenience, the question page always precedes the answer page. Questions are grouped separately from their respective answers. (A "Q" represents a question, while an "A" indicates an answer.)

The questions are current as of November 1993.

CHAPTER

1

Comedy

The Abbott and Costello Show
Syndicated, 1952–54

Q1.   Bud Abbott and Lou Costello, playing out-of-work comedians seeking employment, lived at the Fields Rooming House at 214 Brookline Avenue. How much a week did they pay in rent?

Q2.   To make money, Bud and Lou tried selling hats, roller skates, and "No Peddlers Allowed" signs. They thought they had a chance at the big bucks by going on a TV game show called "Hold That Cuckoo." Lou held that cuckoo (ticking clock) and won the grand prize. What was it?

Q3.   Hillary Brooke played a number of roles on the series, including Lou's girlfriend. In one episode she inherited a haunted castle; in another, a ranch in Texas. What was the name of the ranch?

Q4.   Although landlord Sidney Fields prohibited pets in his apartment house, Lou had a chimpanzee named Bingo. What did Bingo eat for breakfast?

The Addams Family
ABC, 1964–66

Q5.   "Beware of Thing" was posted on the iron gate in front of the Addams house on Cemetery Ridge. Why did the family spell their last name with a second "d"?

The Abbott and Costello Show

A1.   Seven dollars

A2.   A box of bubble gum

A3.   The B-Bar-B Ranch

A4.   Watermelon

The Addams Family

A5.   "It distinguishes us from the embarrassingly famous and historic John Adams and family."

The Addams Family continued

Q6. Gomez, the nattily-dressed father, was independently wealthy but was also an attorney for the defense. What distinguished him from any other attorney?

Q7. The Addams family had strange tastes. What were the three favorite foods of Gomez and his wife, Morticia?

Q8. Morticia's Uncle Fester once worked as an advice-to-the-lovelorn columnist, and his philosophy was "Shoot 'em in the back." What did he call his rifle?

Q9. Gomez's mother, Grandmama Addams, also resided with the family. What high school did she attend?

ALF
NBC, 1986–90

Q10. ALF was an alien who crashed into the garage of the Tanner Family when the frequencies from Willie Tanner's short-wave radio interfered with those of ALF's space ship. ALF, born on the planet Melmac 229 years ago, craved cats (his favorite meal), and loved to eat. How many stomachs did ALF have and what was his body temperature?

Q11. Melmac was destroyed by an explosion, leaving ALF one of the few remaining survivors. What was the motto of the planet?

Q12. Willie was married to Kate. They tied the knot on July 11, 1967. Where did they honeymoon?

Q13. ALF loved Earth TV and believed cartoons reflected real life. He had two favorite TV shows. One was *Gilligan's Island*; what was the other?

A6.   He was responsible for putting more men behind bars than any other lawyer in the U.S.

A7.   Fried yak, fried eyes of newt, and barbecued turtle tips

A8.   Genevieve

A9.   Swamp Town High

ALF

A10.   Eight stomachs; 425 degrees

A11.   "Are you going to finish that sandwich?"

A12.   The Duke of Mist Hotel in Niagara Falls

A13.   *Polka Time*

Alice
CBS, 1976–85

Q14. A dish called Mel's Chili was the special of the day (every day) at Mel's Diner, a roadside eatery in Arizona. It was located on which specific highway?

Q15. Alice, Flo, and Vera were the waitresses who constantly complained that they needed a raise. How much an hour did "cheapskate" Mel Sharples pay them?

All in the Family
CBS, 1971–78

Q16. Archie Bunker believed that credit was the American way of life ("That way you can buy anything you can't afford"). Where was Archie first stationed during "The Big One" (World War II)?

Q17. Although he called his wife, Edith, "Dingbat," he loved her very much. Where did Archie meet Edith?

Q18. When Gloria, their daughter, was born in 1944, Edith and Archie could barely afford to pay the hospital bill. How much did Gloria's birth cost?

Q19. In 1948, when TV was new, Archie and Edith couldn't afford a set. Where did they watch *The Milton Berle Show*?

Q20. While Edith never held a regular nine-to-five job after marrying Archie, she did have one prior to meeting him. Where did she work?

Amen
NBC, 1986–91

Q21. Ernest Frye, the deacon of the First Community Church of Philadelphia, also was an attorney. What words appeared on his office door after his name ("Attorney-at-Law Ernest Frye...")?

Alice

A14.   Bush Highway

A15. $2.90

All in the Family

A16.   Fort Riley, Kansas

A17.   At The Puritan Maid Ice Cream Parlor

A18. $131.50

A19.   From the window of Tupperman's Department Store

A20.   The Hercules Plumbing Company

Amen

A21.   "Where Winning is Everything"

Amen continued

Q22. Thelma, Ernest's daughter, was called the "Undateable" in high school. What school did she attend?

Q23. Although Thelma could not cook, she hosted a TV show called *Thelma's Kitchen*. What company sponsored it?

The Amos 'n' Andy Show
   CBS, 1951–53

Q24. Amos Jones, Andy Brown, and George "Kingfish" Stevens were friends who lived on Lenox Avenue in Manhattan. Amos and Andy resided previously in what Georgia city before "coming up north" to begin new lives?

Q25. Con artist Kingfish sold Andy the cab they used for the Fresh Air Taxi Company of America, Inc. How much did he con out of Andy for it?

Q26. Living by cons was Kingfish's livelihood. What was his favorite activity?

Q27. Sapphire, Kingfish's wife, put up with all of her husband's nonsense. Although they argued constantly, she loved him and was apparently the breadwinner. For what company did Sapphire work?

The Andy Griffith Show
   CBS, 1960–68

Q28. Handing out parking tickets and replacing the lids on garbage cans was part of the job for Sheriff Andy Taylor and his deputy, Barney Fife, in the small town of Mayberry, North Carolina. Andy's experiences as sheriff have been written up in the National Sheriff's magazine. What did the magazine call Andy?

Q29. Andy and Barney were actually cousins and 1945 graduates of what high school?

A22.   West Holmes High

A23.   Bake Rite Flour

The Amos 'n' Andy Show

A24.   Marietta

A25. $340

A26.   Sleeping

A27.   Superfine Brush Company

The Andy Griffith Show

A28.   "The Sheriff Without a Gun"

A29.   Mayfield Union High

The Andy Griffith Show continued

Q30. Aunt Bee raised Andy and claimed that "Andy is meaner than a bear that backed into a beehive when he doesn't eat supper." Andy was most fond of which of Aunt Bee's desserts?

Q31. Opie, Andy's son, had several pets, including a lizard, a dog, and a parakeet. Dinkie was the parakeet's name, but what did Opie call the dog and lizard?

Angie
ABC, 1979–80

Q32. Angie was a hardworking waitress who found her life turned upside down when she married a rich doctor (Brad Benson). Although Angie did not need to work, she continued to do so in what coffee shop?

Q33. Angie's mother, Theresa Falco, ran the family business, the Falco Newsstand. When a better business opportunity came along, she sold the newsstand and purchased what beauty parlor?

Anything but Love
ABC, 1989–92

Q34. Hannah Miller and Marty Gold were lovers who also worked as writers for *Chicago Weekly* magazine. Hannah, a beautiful woman who struggled to maintain her figure, was most proud of her breasts and had a specific name for them. What did she call them?

Q35. Hannah and her best friend, Robin, had known each other since they were five. They also lived in the same apartment building and had a nickname for each other. What was it?

Q36. In the eleventh grade, Hannah and Robin began to think about their futures and made a pact. What was it?

Q37. When Hannah and Marty dined out, they ate at what specific restaurant?

A30. Apple and Butterscotch Pecan Pie

A31. Gulliver the dog; Oscar the lizard

Angie

A32. The Liberty Coffee Shop

A33. Rose's House of Beauty

Anything but Love

A34. "The Girls"

A35. Mrs. Schmenkman

A36. If neither was married by age thirty, each would tell people her husband was with the Witness Protection Program.

A37. Marino's

Anything but Love continued

Q38. Marty enjoyed being with Hannah, but there were times he relished going out with the boys for the kind of entertainment he felt Hannah wouldn't like. What bar did Marty frequent on these occasions?

Baby Talk
ABC, 1991–92

Q39. Maggie Campbell was a single mother struggling to raise her infant son Mickey. Mickey had type AB blood, a rubber ducky named Ralphie, and red Jell-O was his favorite food. What was his favorite song?

Q40. Thinking Mickey had acting talent, Maggie let him audition for the tropical line of baby food for what company?

Q41. When Mary Page Keller replaced Julia Duffy in the role of Maggie, she acquired a job as an accountant at what company?

Q42. James Halbrook was Maggie's romantic interest and the building's super. He is a budding songwriter and composed what TV commercial jingle?

Bachelor Father
CBS/NBC/ABC, 1957–62

Q43. A bachelor's effort to raise his pretty niece after the death of her parents was the focal point of this sitcom. Bentley Gregg was the "Bachelor Father" of the title, a private-practice attorney whose office was located in what Los Angeles building?

Q44. Kelly Gregg was the thirteen-year-old who suddenly became Bentley's responsibility. What school did she attend?

Q45. Kelly's favorite subject in school was math. She and her friends frequented what after-school hangout?

A38.   Dick and Dee's International House of Mud

Baby Talk

A39.   "Muskrat Love"

A40.   Beacon Baby Foods

A41.   Coleman Accounting

A42.   Peachy Time Gum

Bachelor Father

A43.   The Crescent Building

A44.   Beverly Hills High

A45.   Bill's Malt Shop

Benson
ABC, 1979–86

Q46. Benson DuBois was the butler to Gene Gatling, the governor of mythical Capitol City. In what community did Gene reside (the locale of the governor's mansion)?

Q47. Before entering politics, Gene was a paper mill industrialist. What was he famous for at the mill?

Q48. What was the motto of Gov. Gene Gatling's state?

Q49. Gene's personal secretary, Denise, and his press secretary, Peter, married on September 16, 1983. What was Denise's term of endearment for Peter?

Bewitched
ABC, 1964–72

Q50. Samantha and Darrin Stephens lived in Connecticut at 1164 Morning Glory Circle. On what days were the trash pickups?

Q51. When Samantha, a comely witch, had a craving for food, what was the only meal that would satisfy her?

Q52. Sam's beautiful cousin, Serena, called herself "The Goddess of Love." Of what club was Serena a member (she was also the entertainment chairperson)?

Q53. Larry Tate was Darrin's gray-haired boss at the McMahon and Tate Ad Agency. What did Serena call Larry?

Q54. Samantha's Aunt Clara was somewhat addled and was famous for her prized collection of what?

Benson

A46.   Lawrence County

A47.   His bunkhouse biscuits

A48.   "If it's not broken, don't fix it."

A49.   "Bunny Wabbitt Face"

Bewitched

A50.   Tuesday and Friday

A51.   Ringtail pheasant

A52.   The Cosmos Club

A53.   "Peter Cotton Top"

A54.   Doorknobs

Blossom
NBC, 1991–

Q55. Blossom Russo is the perfect combination "of a little sugar and a lot of spice." Although she is only thirteen, her brother Joey calls her a borderline babe—"You're in the honor society, you play the trumpet, but you haven't been visited by the hooter fairy yet." Still a kid, she sleeps with what famous TV-character doll by her side?

Q56. Blossom and her friend, Six, attend Tyler High School and love to dance. Although Blossom dances for obvious reasons, it is not the same case for Six. Why does she dance?

Q57. Anthony, Blossom's older brother, had a drug problem for four years but is now recovering. He first worked for Fatty's Pizza Parlor, then as an emergency medical technician. Who was the first celebrity he assisted?

Q58. Blossom's younger brother, Joey, believes the sun is the other side of the moon and, according to her, "if the dorks had a navy he'd be their admiral." Blossom feels that Joey has only one talent. What is it?

Q59. The family has a cat that though rarely seen is often mentioned. What is its name?

Q60. When a producer came up with an idea for a series about the Russos, what was the show originally called and what was it finally changed to?

Bob
CBS, 1992–93

Q61. Mad Dog, "Mankind's Best Friend," was the comic book creation of Bob McKay, a cartoonist for Ace Comics. What company owned Ace Comics?

Q62. Bob created Mad Dog in 1964 (he drew the concept on a napkin) and sold the idea to a publisher. It never caught on and was yanked after the twelfth issue. How many copies of the first issue were sold?

Blossom

A55.   ALF

A56.   "To get all sweaty and dizzy and see stars."

A57.   Justine Bateman, when she fell and injured her elbow

A58.   Drinking Pepsi through his nose

A59.   Scruffy

A60.   First "The Russos," then "Everything's Coming Up Rosie"

Bob

A61.   American-Canadian Transcontinental Communications

A62.   Nine

Bob continued

Q63. Mad Dog wore blue tights with an orange M on his chest. He also had two human assistants. Who were they?

Q64. Before her job as Bob's colorist, Trisha, his daughter, worked as a "wench waitress" at what pub?

Q65. The owner and publisher of Ace Comics was never seen, but his voice was heard over the speaker phone and his staff lived in fear of him. Who belonged to this "voice of terror"?

The Bob Newhart Show
CBS, 1972–78

Q66. Bob Hartley was a psychologist who lived with his wife, Emily, a grammar school vice principal, in Apartment 523 of a building owned by what company?

Q67. When in need of extra money, Bob took a job as an insurance salesman for a company whose motto was "We gotta insure these guys." Name the company?

Q68. Emily first taught third grade at Gorman Elementary School, then became the vice principal where?

Q69. Howard Borden, Bob's neighbor, was originally a 747 navigator. When he was replaced by a computer he found work with what airline?

Q70. Bob's secretary, Carol, lived in Apartment 7 of an unnamed building. When the doorbell rang, a tape recording of a barking dog was activated. What had Carol named the dog?

Bosom Buddies
ABC, 1980–82

Q71. Kip and Henry worked at an ad agency in Manhattan, but lived in a women-only hotel named the Susan B. Anthony. What was the name of the agency where they toiled?

A63. Penny and Buddy

A64. The Keg and Cleaver

A65. Mr. TerHorst

The Bob Newhart Show

A66. Skyline Management Corporation

A67. Loggers Casualty Insurance

A68. Tracy Grammar School

A69. EDS (European Delivery Service)

A70. Lobo

Bosom Buddies

A71. Livingston, Gentry, and Mishkin

Bosom Buddies continued

Q72. In order to reside at the Susan B. Anthony, Henry and Kip had to dress as women. The clothes they used for this masquerade were from what clients of the agency's?

Q73. When Kip and Henry, and their coworker, Amy Cassidy, quit their jobs, they opened their own ad agency when they purchased a bankrupt commercial production studio. What did they name their company?

Q74. Kip and Henry were longtime friends who had lived in Shaker Heights near Cleveland. What school did they attend?

The Brady Bunch
ABC, 1969–74

Q75. After marrying and forming the Brady Bunch, Mike and Carol set up housekeeping on Clinton Avenue in Los Angeles. Mike designed the house. How many bedrooms and bathrooms did it have?

Q76. In the opening theme, the Bradys (and Alice the housekeeper) were seen in a tic-tac-toe board. Jan, Alice, and Peter were in the middle squares from left to right. Who occupied the top and bottom squares, left to right?

Q77. Marcia and Jan Brady both attended Westdale High School and worked after school at what ice cream parlor?

Q78. When Jan, the middle girl, felt she was not as pretty as Marcia, she pretended to have a boyfriend. What did she call him?

Q79. Cindy, the youngest of the girls, had a Kitty Carry-All doll and two pet rabbits. What did she call the rabbits?

Q80. Greg, the oldest of the boys, formed a singing group called the Brady Six with his brothers and sisters and tried to break into the music business on his own. What name did he use?

A72.   Blouse City and Dresses for Women

A73.   60 Seconds Street

A74.   Edgar Allen Poe High

The Brady Bunch

A75.   Four bedrooms, two bathrooms

A76.   Top: Marcia, Carol, Greg; bottom: Cindy, Mike, Bobby

A77.   Hanson's

A78.   George Glass

A79.   Romeo and Juliet

A80.   Johnny Bravo

The Brady Bunch continued

Q81. Joan of Arc was Cindy's hero; Jesse James was Bobby's. What real person did middle boy Peter mention as being his hero?

Q82. It turned his sisters' hair orange, but Bobby, the youngest Brady thought he could make a million dollars by selling what product?

Bridget Loves Bernie
CBS, 1972–73

Q83. Bridget Fitzgerald was Catholic; Bernie Steinberg was Jewish. They met, fell in love, married, and set up housekeeping in an apartment over Steinberg's Delicatessen on Manhattan's Lower East Side. Bernie drove a taxi, and at what school did Bridget teach?

Q84. Bernie's parents, Sam and Sophie, owned the deli over which Bridget and Bernie lived. Bridget's rich parents were Walter and Amy. What company did Walter own?

Q85. IC-56 was the license plate of the cab driven by Bernie. What was his cab number?

Captain Nice
NBC, 1967

Q86. When he tried to join the army, they burned his draft card. When he enrolled in a self-defense course, "They said I should carry an axe." He was afraid of girls, was ordinary and didn't stand out. He was Carter Nash, a nebbishy police chemist who invented a liquid that transformed him into Captain Nice, a daring crime fighter. Where did Carter get the inspiration to name his alter ego?

Q87. After drinking his invention, something happened before lightning struck and transformed Carter into Captain Nice. What was it?

A81.   George Washington

A82.   Neat and Natural Hair Tonic

Bridget Loves Bernie

A83.   Immaculate Heart Academy

A84.   Global Investments

A85.   Cab number 12

Captain Nice

A86.   From the initials on his belt buckle—C.N.

A87.   Carter hiccupped

Captain Nice continued

Q88. Carter's mother knew that her son was the heroic Captain Nice, but his father was not aware of Carter's alias and not even particularly aware of Carter. When Mr. Nash couldn't remember Carter's name, what did he call him?

Car 54, Where Are You?
NBC, 1961–63

Q89. Gunther Toody and Francis Muldoon were police officers with the 53rd Precinct in the Bronx. They rode together in patrol car 54 and were members of what fraternity?

Q90. Francis was single while Gunther was married to the always nagging Lucille. What was Lucille's maiden name?

Q91. Francis lived with his mother and sister, Peggy. Mrs. Muldoon had a fascination with what movie idol after whom she named her son?

Q92. The henpecked Leo Schnauser was also an officer with the 53rd. Sylvia, his wife, was always suspicious when he went out for a night with Toody and Muldoon. What did Sylvia think Leo was doing on these occasions?

Charles in Charge
Syndicated, 1987–90

Q93. Charles was the live-in housekeeper to the Powell family in New Jersey while he attended college. What was its name?

Q94. While Charles was majoring in education, his friend, Buddy, had been told that aptitude tests indicated that he was best qualified for jury duty. What was Buddy's real first name?

A88.   Spot

Car 54, Where Are You?

A89.   The Brotherhood Club

A90.   Hasselwhite

A91.   Francis X. Bushman

A92.   Having a secret affair with Marilyn Monroe

Charles in Charge

A93.   Copeland College

A94.   Buddence

Charles in Charge continued

Q95. Buddy lived in the college dorm with his pet lizard Lloyd, and ant, Arlo. As a kid, Buddy had not only a hand puppet he called Handie but a dog, also. What did he call the pooch?

Q96. Jamie, the oldest of the Powell children, was an exceptionally pretty teenager. Her good looks got her a role in what TV commercial?

Q97. While Jamie was growing into a beautiful woman, her father still saw her as a little girl. What did he call her?

Q98. Sarah, the middle child, was sensitive and longed to be a writer. Ross was the name of her pet turtle. What was her favorite doll's name?

Q99. The mythical college Charles attended had a mascot. What was it?

The Charmings
ABC, 1987–88

Q100. When told by her magic mirror that she was not the fairest of all, the evil queen, Lillian, cast a spell on Snow White. The spell backfired and suspended Lillian, Snow White, Snow's husband, Eric Charming, and their children, Thomas and Cory, a thousand years. They awoke to a new life in 1987, and Snow White now worked as a fashion designer, with Eric a children's story book author. What was the name of the first book he wrote?

Q101. Lillian—maiden name was Lipschitz—suffered from P.M.S. (Post Magic Syndrome) once every twenty-eight years, and had a pet thing (an unknown creature) and a crow. Name either the thing or the crow.

Q102. Other pets in the Charming household were Eric's horse and Thomas and Cory's lizard. Give the name for either one.

A95.   Kitty

A96.   Banana Cream Shampoo and Hair Lotion

A97.   "Little Scooter"

A98.   Rebecca

A99.   Mr. Hobbs, the goat

The Charmings

A100.   *The Four Billy Goats Gruff*

A101.   Muffin was the thing; Quoth was the crow.

A102.   The horse was Gendel; the lizard was Spike.

Cheers
NBC, 1982–93

Q103. The bar at 112½ Beacon Street in Boston was Cheers, "the place where everybody knows your name." What was the legal capacity according to a notice that was posted above the door?

Q104. When Sam Malone, the current bar owner, was a ballplayer, he found something that he used as a good luck charm. What was it?

Q105. Diane Chambers was the first barmaid. In addition to being an art student and substitute teacher at Boston University, she held two other jobs. Name one of them.

Q106. Rebecca Howe was part of the large corporation that purchased Cheers after Sam originally sold it. What was her computer password for the corporation?

Q107. Rebecca often wondered why she took the job as the bar's business manager as it caused her nothing but aggravation. Watching what favorite TV show usually calmed her?

Q108. Ernie Pantusso, called Coach, was Sam's original bartender. He also had another nickname as pitching coach for the Boston Red Sox. What was it?

Q109. Carla was Sam's nasty, wisecracking, oft-married waitress. She attended St. Clete's School for Wayward Girls, and this is probably the most difficult question in the book: What was Carla's full name?

Q110. At what bar did Carla work before Sam hired her?

Q111. When she was a kid, Diane's father called her "Muffin" because she was sweet; as a kid Carla was also called "Muffin" by her brothers. Why?

Q112. Bar regular Cliff Claven was a mailman assigned to the South Central Branch. Besides the dog on his route, Cliff feared one thing because it put an extra strain on him. What was it?

Cheers

A103. 75 people

A104. A bottle cap

A105. Salesgirl at the Third Eye Bookstore or checker at Hurley's Market

A106. Sweet Baby

A107. *Spenser: For Hire*

A108. "Red" (not because he had red hair but because he once read a book)

A109. Carla Maria Victoria Angelina Teresa Appollonia Lozupone Tortelli LeBec

A110. The Broken Spoke

A111. Because her brothers stuffed her ears with yeast and tried to bake her face.

A112. The day the Sears catalogue came out

Cheers continued

Q113. Norm Peterson was another regular who loved to eat, drink, and run up large bar tabs. Married to the unseen Vera, he was a CPA. What was Norm's real first name?

Q114. Woody Boyd became Sam's bartender after Coach's death. He was born in Hanover, Indiana, and was known for inventing what game?

Q115. Bar regular Frasier Crane is a psychiatrist who considered himself "the solver of all things personal," and conducted self-help seminars that cost $350. What did he call them?

Q116. "Frost Warning" was the term Cliff uses when Frasier's wife, Lilith, entered the bar. Lilith was also a psychiatrist who "rides the roost in her bra and panties," according to Frasier. What book had Lilith written that made her famous?

Clarissa Explains It All
Nickelodeon, 1991–

Q117. Clarissa Darling is a thirteen-year-old who doesn't particularly like her name. "Anything without a last name would have been great" she says, "but no one asked me." Clarissa lives at 464 Shadow Lane in what town?

Q118. Many people have a dog for protection, but not our Clarissa. She has a pet alligator she calls Elvis, who lives in a small plastic pool in Clarissa's room. What has she named the pool?

Q119. Clarissa's mother, Janet, is a vitamin freak and health food nut whose Zucchini lentil surprise is her favorite dinner. What is her favorite dessert?

Q120. Marshall, Clarissa's father, is an architect. By what term of endearment does he call Clarissa?

A113. Hilary

A114. Hide Bob's Pants

A115. "The Crane Train to Mental Well Being"

A116. *Good Girls/Bad Boys*

Clarissa Explains It All

A117. Baxter Beach

A118. The Heartbreak Hotel

A119. Carob pudding cake with whipped tofu topping

A120. "Sport"

The Cosby Show
NBC, 1984–92

Q121. The Huxtable Family lived at 10 Stigwood Avenue in Brooklyn. Cliff, the father, was an obstetrician who worked from his home and at two hospitals. One was Corinthian Hospital. What was the other?

Q122. Both Cliff and his wife, Clair, attended Hillman College in Georgia. Clair majored in law and worked for what firm?

Q123. Attending Hillman College was a Huxtable tradition, but Sondra, the oldest child, was the first to break it. It cost Cliff and Clair $79,648.72 to send their daughter to what college?

Q124. Denise, the second born, was the most troublesome of the Huxtable kids. She quit Hillman after three semesters and had a couple of jobs before marrying Martin Kendall. Name one of the two jobs Denise held.

Q125. Cliff and Clair's only son, Theo, was the second to break tradition when he attended NYU. In high school Theo was a member of the wrestling team. What did they call him?

Q126. Vanessa, the fourth child, also broke tradition (she attended the University of Philadelphia). What was the name of the rock group Vanessa joined while in high school?

Q127. Impish Rudy was the youngest Huxtable. Vanilla was her favorite flavor of ice cream and she played on a Pee Wee League football team. She had a teddy bear and a goldfish. Rudy called the goldfish Lamont, but what was the name of her teddy bear?

Q128. Sondra married Elvin, a medical student who eventually became a doctor, although he almost gave it up for a psychological reason. What was it?

The Cosby Show

A121. Children's Hospital

A122. Greentree, Bradley, and Dexter

A123. Princeton

A124. Salesgirl at the Wilderness Store; assistant to the executive assistant at Blue Wave Records

A125. "Monster Man Huxtable"

A126. The Lipsticks

A127. Bobo

A128. He had a problem charging people for medical help.

Davis Rules
CBS, 1991–92

Q129. Dwight Davis, a widower, lived in Seattle with his children, Robbie, Charlie, and Ben, and his father, Gunny, at 631 Evergreen. He taught math, science, and history and was also the principal of what grammar school?

Q130. Dwight loved golf, but played only three times a year. He hung out at what golfing store where he was called a "browse-aholic"?

Q131. Gunny, whose real name was William Davis, got the nickname during his service with the marines. What did he call the USMC?

Q132. Gunny now cared for the family. A great cook, he could make top-notch stew out of what?

Q133. Gwen, Dwight's effervescent sister, came to live with the family in second-season episodes. For what radio station did Gwen work?

Dear John
NBC, 1988–92

Q134. John Lacey one day returned home from work to find a Dear John letter from his wife, Wendy. How long were they married before she left him?

Q135. In an attempt to adjust to the single life, John joined the One-on-One Club. On what night did the club hold its meetings?

Q136. Now living in Apartment 42 on Woodhaven Boulevard in Manhattan, John cared for the three cats of his unseen ninety-two-year-old neighbor. Name the pets.

Q137. Pretty club member Mary Beth Sutton had been a homecoming queen and always expected the best to happen. For what airline magazine did she work?

Davis Rules

A129.   Pomahac Elementary School

A130.   Par for the Course

A131.   "Uncle Sam's Miserable Children"

A132.   Roadkill

A133.   KPLG

Dear John

A134.   Ten years

A135.   Fridays

A136.   Snuffy, Fluffy, and Snowball

A137.   *Above the Clouds*

Dear John continued

Q138.   Ralph Drang, the always-worried Lincoln Tunnel toll-booth attendant, lived by himself and had decorated his bedroom with wallpaper from what famous TV show?

Q139.   Overconfident schemer and con artist Kirk Morris lost his wife to another woman. What was the name of the catering company that he and his friend, Denise, operated?

December Bride
CBS, 1954–59

Q140.   Lily Ruskin, a young-at-heart sixty-year-old widow, lived with her married daughter, Ruth Henshaw, and son-in-law Matt at 728 Elm Street in Westwood, California. What was unique about the block on which they resided?

Q141.   Lily sought to help people either in person or through the newspaper column she wrote for the *Los Angeles Gazette*. What was her column called?

Q142.   Next-door neighbor Peter Porter claimed that "I'm not henpecked, I'm buzzardpecked." He was, of course, referring to his never-seen wife, Gladys. What did Pete say were the symbols of his marriage?

Q143.   When the show *Pete and Gladys* was spun off into a series of its own, one of the characters Pete mentioned on *December Bride*—their daughter—was not used. What was her name?

Delta
ABC, 1992–93

Q144.   Patsy Cline was the idol of Delta Bishop, a Mississippi hairdresser who dreamt of becoming a country singer. Where did Delta work before moving to Nashville to pursue her dream?

A138. *Star Trek*

A139. Cuisine by Kirk

December Bride

A140. As Matt said: "It is lined with Palm Trees. One block over is Palm Street which is lined with Elm Trees."

A141. "Tips for Housewives"

A142. "A padlock, chains, and a straightjacket."

A143. Linda

Delta

A144. Mona's House of Hair

Delta *continued*

Q145. In Nashville, Delta acquired a job at the Green Lantern, a bar where Patsy Cline supposedly sang. It was owned by Darden Towe, a former stockbroker who bought it as a way of escaping his hectic life. After his marriage broke up, he became its full-time operator and wrote "an awful gladiator novel." What was the name of the work?

Q146. Delta resided in an apartment over the garage of a house owned by her cousin, Lavonne. At what beauty salon did Lavonne work?

Designing Women
CBS, 1986–93

Q147. Sisters Julia and Suzanne Sugarbaker owned a chic interior decorating firm in Atlanta. From what store do they buy their goods?

Q148. Julia was the more sophisticated sister. "To get a vacation from being myself" (to find her spiritual self), Julia changed her name to Giselle and sang at what nightclub?

Q149. Totally self-absorbed Suzanne flaunted her sexuality to get what she wanted. Although objecting to this, Julia was very proud of Suzanne for winning what beauty title?

Q150. Charlene Frazier was the office manager at Sugarbakers, but took a second job to help pay the bills. What was her other job?

Q151. Mary Jo Shively, the divorced mother of two, was the firm's buyer. Although her dog was never seen, she talked about him frequently. What was his name?

Q152. Allison Sugarbaker, Julia's cousin, came on the scene in 1991 when Suzanne took off for Japan. Allison sobbed at everything and suffered from what she called O.P.D. What was this?

A145. *I, Dardenius*

A146. Thelma's Hairdressers

Designing Women

A147. Fabric World

A148. The Blue Note Cafe

A149. Miss Georgia World of 1976

A150. Salesgirl for Kemper Cosmetics

A151. Brownie

A152. Obnoxious Personality Disorder

Designing Women continued

Q153. When Charlene moved to England, her down-home sister, Carlene, joined the firm. Where did Carlene work before Sugarbakers?

Q154. Anthony Bouvier is the ex-con who became the firm's delivery man. Where did he serve time for his part in a liquor store robbery?

Q155. During the series' final season, Anthony married a beautiful showgirl named Etienne Toussant, who worked at the Tropicana Resort and Casino and referred to Anthony as "Tony, 'cause he's my tiger." What did Etienne like to be called?

The Dick Van Dyke Show
CBS, 1961–66

Q156. Rob Petrie met Laura Meeker while stationed at the Camp Crowder Army Base in Joplin, Missouri. He was a sergeant; she was a USO girl. While doing a song and dance number together, Rob, who was wearing combat boots, stepped on Laura's foot and broke her toes. Name the song to which they were performing.

Q157. Rob and Laura married while he was still in the service and set up housekeeping first on the army base, then in Ohio when Rob was discharged. He found work as a disc jockey at what radio station?

Q158. After an interview with TV star Alan Brady, Rob got a job as his head writer in New York City. *The Alan Brady Show* was rated number one in Liberia; what was its ranking in the U.S.?

Q159. Several of Alan Brady's companies paid the bills. Rob got his checks from the Ishomor Company; the show's band was paid by Brady Lady (named after Alan's wife). What company, named for Alan's mother-in-law, paid Rob's fellow writers, Sally Rogers and Buddy Sorrell?

A153. Ray Flat's Flatbed Furniture Store

A154. Cell Block D of Atlanta State Prison

A155. "E.T."

The Dick Van Dyke Show

A156. "You Wonderful You"

A157. WOFF

A158. Number 17

A159. Barracuda, Ltd.

The Dick Van Dyke Show *continued*

Q160. Rob and Laura lived in New Rochelle, New York. In the basement of their house, behind some loose bricks in back of the furnace, Laura hid something from Rob. What was it?

Q161. One night, when Rob couldn't sleep, he decided to count the roses on his bedroom wallpaper. How many roses were there?

Q162. Before the birth of Rob and Laura's son, Ritchie, everybody suggested a name for him. Laura wanted Robert or Roberta; Rob, Laura or Lawrence. Sally suggested Valentino ("I was saving it for a parakeet, but you can have it"), and show producer Mel Cooley suggested three names: Allen, Allan, and Alan. What name did Buddy suggest?

Q163. At Herbie's Hiawatha Lodge, one could catch Buddy and Sally performing a comical song and dance routine. By what names did they bill themselves?

Q164. Buddy once had his own show, *Buddy's Bag*, and also worked as a writer on *The Billy Barrows Show*. What is Buddy's real first name?

Q165. Sally was single and looking for Mr. Right. She dated Herman Glimshire, a mama's boy, and had two cats. One was named Mr. Henderson; what did she call the other?

A Different World
NBC, 1987–93

Q166. Hillman College in Georgia was not just a tough school, "it was a butt breaker." Cliff and Clair Huxtable's daughter, Denise, enrolled there, but couldn't seem to achieve the *As* and *Bs* she got in high school. What was her grade average after three semesters (when she dropped out)?

Q167. While Denise didn't keep track of the checks she wrote ("I'm in college now. I'm busy, I have responsibilities"), she did bring something to cheer up the dorm room she shared with Maggie and Jaleesa. What was it?

A160. Her old love letters from high school boyfriend Joe Coogan

A161. 382½

A162. "Exit. If the kid is an actor, it'll be in every theater in the country."

A163. Gilbert and Solomon

A164. Maurice

A165. Mr. Diefenthaler

A Different World

A166. 1.7 (One point seven)

A167. A deer lamp with lights on the antlers

A Different World *continued*

Q168. Maggie, an army brat, left Hillman at the same time as Denise when her father was transferred overseas. While Denise had an undecided major, Maggie was determined to become something. What was her major?

Q169. Whitley Gilbert was one of the most beautiful girls at Hillman. She hailed from Richmond, Virginia, where her father was a judge, and her passion was art and shopping. Very proud of the fact that her beauty allowed her to steal men from other girls, vain Whitley would use a bar of soap only once and could not stand anyone else touching or wearing her clothes. She would not under any circumstances eat what food—or allow anyone to eat it in her presence?

Q170. He wore "those funny-looking flip-down sunglasses that drive you crazy" and he hit on almost every girl in sight. He was Dwayne Wayne, who pursued a math degree. Dwayne's middle name was Creofus; but when he had a talk show on the school radio station, what did he call himself?

Diff'rent Strokes
NBC/ABC, 1978–86

Q171. Although the daughter of a rich father (Phillip Drummond), Kimberly wanted to make money on her own. She supplemented her weekly ten-dollar allowance by taking an after-school job at what fast-food store in Manhattan?

Q172. Arnold and Willis Jackson were the two brothers Phillip adopted. Arnold, the younger, more mischievous one, had a ratty old doll named Homer, a cricket named Lucky, and a goldfish. What did he call the fish?

Q173. Arnold loved model railroading and video games. He had his railroad empire set up in his bedroom and he was the champ at what game at the Video Arcade?

Q174. While he attended a number of different grammar schools, one thing plagued Arnold no matter which one it was—the school bully. What was the bully's name?

A168.   Journalism

A169.   Cheese

A170.   Darryl Walker

Diff'rent Strokes

A171.   The Hula Hut

A172.   Abraham

A173.   "Space Sucker"

A174.   The Gooch

Diff'rent Strokes continued

Q175. As a kid, older brother Willis had a doll named Wendy Wetems. He also had a favorite expression ("Say what?") and he formed a rock band that featured his sister and his girlfriend, Charlene, as lead singers. What was the name of the band?

Dinosaurs
ABC, 1991–93

Q176. It was the year 60,000,003 B.C. and dinosaurs had come out of the forests to marry and raise a family. Human beings of this era were portrayed as a less-intelligent life form. One dinosaur family, the Sinclairs, had a pet human (a cavegirl). What was her name?

Q177. Earl Sinclair, wife Fran, and children Charlene and Robbie lived as suburbanites in the town of Pangaea. What was the symbol of supremacy in a dinosaur house?

Q178. In the first episode, the family was blessed with another mouth to feed when Baby Sinclair was hatched. The entire household was shocked when Baby spoke his first word (a gutter word in this world). What was it?

Q179. Baby seemed to recognize everybody in the family but his father, Earl, and hit him on the head with a frying pan, saying, "Not the mama!" By what brand of pan did Earl get hit over the head?

Q180. Fran shopped for food at the Swamp Basket and prepared such dishes as waffle meat pancakes. What was the family's favorite breakfast cereal?

Q181. Earl and Fran had been married for nineteen years when the series began. Where did Earl keep the marriage license?

Q182. The Job Wizard decreed what job each dinosaur will hold and the Elders ruled the land. From where did the Elders rule?

Q183. Wars had been started over it and it was a rare treat, but it was a favorite dinosaur snack. What was it?

A175.   The Afro Desiacs

Dinosaurs

A176.   Sparky

A177.   Possession of the TV remote control

A178.   "Smoo"

A179.   A Myman Frying Pan

A180.   Boo Boo Bears Cereal

A181.   Under the TV to balance it

A182.   The Cave of Destiny

A183.   Pistachio nuts

Dobie Gillis
CBS, 1959–63

Q184. Herbert T. Gillis and his wife, Winnie, owned the Gillis Grocery Store, where their girl-crazy teenage son, Dobie, worked. Known as a cheapskate, Herbert was voted "the citizen most likely to hang on to his last dollar." He frequented the Scarpitta Barber Shop and was a member of what fraternity?

Q185. Dobie was most famous for his infatuation with the beautiful but vain Thalia Menninger. Dobie was usually penniless, but Thalia has plans to improve him so he could make "oodles and oodles of money." What was Thalia's favorite perfume that, at $18 an ounce, Dobie couldn't afford to buy her?

Q186. Maynard G. Krebs, Dobie's bearded beatnik friend, loved to play the bongos and was a hip jazz fan. Where did Maynard hang out (where he played records so much that he wore out the grooves)?

Q187. Maynard had a weekly allowance of thirty-five cents and loved to watch the movie *The Monster That Devoured Cleveland*. He also liked to drive but failed his driving test how many times in how many years?

Q188. Maynard had the world's largest collection of tinfoil, three cousins named Flopsy, Mopsy, and Cottontail, and a stuffed armadillo. What was the name of his pet critter?

Q189. Chatsworth Osborne, Jr., the filthy rich, spoiled heir to the Osborne banking fortune, called his mother "Mumsey." What did she call him?

Q190. Chatsworth had type R (for Royal) blood and belonged to what club at S. Peter Pryor College?

Dobie Gillis

A184. The Benevolent Order of the Bison Lodge

A185. "MMMM"

A186. Riff Ryan's Music Store

A187. Forty-six times in six years

A188. Herman

A189. "You nasty boy"

A190. The Silver Spoons Club

The Donna Reed Show
ABC, 1958–66

Q191. Dr. Alex Stone, his wife, Donna, and their children, Mary and Jeff, lived in the small town of Hilldale in the fifth district. What distinguished this house from the others on the block?

Q192. A pediatrician, Alex was just an intern when he met and married Donna Mullinger, a nurse. During their honeymoon Alex heard one song so many times that he came to hate it. What song was it?

Q193. Daughter Mary was three years older than Jeff, hung out with her friends at Kelzey's Malt Shop, and enjoyed dancing at the Round Robin. What size dress did Mary wear?

Q194. As a kid Jeff put on puppet shows for his friends. What was the name of the puppet he used?

Q195. Jeff was a member of the Bobcats football team and his favorite TV show was *Gunbutt*. What product sponsored the show?

The Duck Factory
NBC, 1984

Q196. Buddy Winkler Productions produced a Saturday morning cartoon series called *The Dippy Duck Show*. The network that aired the series was not named and put it on for only one reason. What was it?

Q197. The daring Dippy, a duck who battled for right, had a number of enemies. Name one of them.

Q198. The beautiful Sherry Jurwalski was a topless Las Vegas ice skater who married Buddy Winkler and inherited the Winkler empire when he died three weeks later. What did Aggie, the animation director, call Sherry?

The Donna Reed Show

A191.   A carob tree on the front lawn

A192.   "Melancholy Baby"

A193.   Eight

A194.   Bongo

A195.   Happy Gum—the All-Purpose Chewing Gum

The Duck Factory

A196.   They got it cheap.

A197.   Irving the Terrible and Rotten Renaldo

A198.   The Widow Winkler

Duffy's Tavern
NBC, 1954

Q199. Duffy's Tavern was where "the elite meet to eat" and where, with a beer, the free lunch costs fifteen cents. The Feinschmecker Brewery of Greater Staten Island serviced the tavern. What beer did Duffy order?

Q200. Located on a shabby section of New York's Third Avenue, Duffy's Tavern had a caring attitude about its customers ("We don't roll customers until they're drunk," said Archie the bartender). But the tavern also lost money on rainy nights. Why?

Q201. Simple-minded Clifton Finnegan, Archie's friend, collected cigar bands as a hobby and never married because of what happened to his parents—"They became a mother and father." Archie also never married. What was his reason?

Empty Nest
NBC, 1988–

Q202. A widower living with his daughters, Carol and Barbara, at 1755 Fairview Road in Miami Beach, Dr. Harry Weston had an office at the Community Medical Center. From what medical school did Harry graduate?

Q203. Harry bought his medical supplies from the Radacine Medical Supplies Company. What brand of bandages did he use for his patients?

Q204. Oldest daughter Carol laughs too loud, is a klutz at sewing, and has a dream of opening a self-help book shop. While she worked at a number of jobs (ten before the series began), she had two we know of—the assistant director of the University of Miami Rare Books Library and a catering business she later began. What is the name of her company?

Q205. Carol is good with money and has fat attacks each spring. She is also a member of what support group?

Duffy's Tavern

A199.   The Weehawken Lager Beer Nectar

A200.   "Who wants to go out and lay in the gutter?"

A201.   "I wanted my wife to have everything—money, a mansion, a big car, and a yacht, but I ain't found the right dame yet."

Empty Nest

A202.   Bedford Medical School

A203.   Starbright Bandages

A204.   Elegant Epicure

A205.   Adult Children of Perfectly Fine Parents

Empty Nest *continued*

Q206. Sister Barbara is terrible with money and works as a police officer. Her favorite comic strip is *Beetle Bailey* and she and her father wrote a book. What did they call it?

Q207. Barbara collects backscratchers and uses what anti-perspirant? (It's "the official antiperspirant of the Miss Junior Teen USA Pageant.")

Q208. As kids, Carol and Barbara attended Camp Weemawalk. Barbara was called "Swim Like a Fish." What was Carol called?

Q209. When Kristy McNichol (who played Barbara) left the series due to manic depression, Harry's previously unseen youngest daughter, Emily, was brought on. What college was Emily attending?

Q210. Laverne Todd, Harry's brash nurse-receptionist, is from Hickory, Arkansas. To get home for visits, Laverne takes a plane to Little Rock, then what private charter plane to Hickory?

Q211. To protect her job, Laverne has a secret decoder to unscramble her filing system. Her maiden name is Higbee, she reads the *National Inquisitor*, and she wears what shade of lipstick?

Q212. The obnoxious, food-pilfering Charlie Dietz is Harry's neighbor. Charlie considers himself a ladies' man and is the fifth assistant purser on what luxury liner?

Evening Shade
CBS, 1990–

Q213. Wood Newton is the football coach of the Mules, the high school team in Evening Shade, Arkansas. He is married to Ava, the town's prosecuting attorney, and they are the parents of three children (Molly, Will, and Taylor). What was Wood's nickname when he played football at Evening Shade High?

A206. *Jumpy Goes to the Hospital*

A207. "Zesty"

A208. "Stay in Tent"

A209. The Hollyoak Girls School

A210. Dwayne's Plane

A211. Passion Pink

A212. *The Ocean Queen*

Evening Shade

A213. Thumper

Evening Shade continued

Q214. Wood next attended the University of Arkansas and became a quarterback for the Pittsburgh Steelers. He wore jersey number 22 and had what nickname?

Q215. Ava has been married to Wood for fifteen years. As a kid, she was called "Chubby" Evans, and it took her two years to lose the weight. In the house she shares with Wood, Ava has one cherished possession. What is it?

Q216. Molly is eleven years old, wears a size 5½ shoe, and attends Evening Shade Grammar School. Her favorite movie is *The Wizard of Oz* and she entered the Little Miss Evening Shade Contest (she lost when she fell attempting to wear high heels). When Molly began to fill out, she wanted a particular bra. Which one was it?

Q217. Harlan Eldridge, the town doctor, and his wife, Merleen, live on an estate they call Tara. What is the name of Harlan's boat?

Q218. Merleen believes that she exudes sexuality and is a magnet to perverts. She is most proud of three pictures that hang on the wall of her home. What are they of?

Q219. Nub Oliver delivers the town's newspaper from his little wagon. He claims to have seen every movie that was ever made and has named his paper wagon after one of them. What is it called?

F Troop
ABC, 1965–67

Q220. Fort Courage was an army fort in Kansas (1866) that had been named after the distinguished general Sam Courage. Before Capt. Wilton Parmenter became its commander, who was in charge of the fort?

Q221. Prior to his promotion as captain, Parmenter was a private with the Union Quartermaster Corps. What were his duties?

A214.   Clutch

A215.   Her antique bathroom window

A216.   The Littlest Angel Bra

A217.   Tara of the Sea

A218.   Billy Graham, an American Indian, and Tom Selleck

A219.   Chariot of Fire

F Troop

A220.   "Cannonball" Bill McCormick

A221.   Doing the officers' laundry

F Troop continued

Q222. O'Rourke Enterprises was the not-exactly-legal business venture run by crafty Sgt. Morgan O'Rourke and his vice president, Corp. Randolph Agarn. Besides the Fort Courage Saloon, what else comprises O'Rourke Enterprises?

Q223. When Agarn bought his way out of the army to manage a somewhat anachronistic rock group called the Bedbugs, O'Rourke organized his own band to discourage Agarn and get him to reenlist. What was O'Rourke's group called?

Q224. Comely Wrangler Jane owned Wrangler Jane's, the combination off-post post office and general store. In love with Wilton, she had set her sights on him and tried to wrangle a proposal. Jane could shoot, rope, and trick-ride a horse. What was the name of her horse?

The Facts of Life
NBC, 1979–88

Q225. Blair, Jo, Tootie, and Natalie were four teenagers who attended the Eastland School for Girls in Peekskill, New York. Blair, the most beautiful girl at the academy, was conceited, a snob, and heir to the Warner Textile Industries. She won a number of awards at Eastland. Name at least two of the three awards that were mentioned.

Q226. Blair's complete opposite was Jo, a poor Bronx girl with a tough exterior, who was at Eastland on a scholarship and was always in need of extra money. What was the name of the business she and fellow students Tootie and Natalie tried to launch?

Q227. Tootie, the youngest of the girls, wanted to become an actress. In what show did she have the lead that made her the first black girl in the school's history to play the role?

Q228. Natalie had ambitions to become a journalist and worked as a reporter for the *Peekskill Press*. What was the title of her first article while at Eastland?

A222. The International Trading Company

A223. The Termites

A224. Pecos

The Facts of Life

A225. Eastland Harvest Queen; Most Naturally Blonde; and Small Business Woman's Association Award (for inventing contour top sheets)

A226. Mama Rosa's Original Bronx Pizza, Inc.

A227. Juliet in *Romeo and Juliet*

A228. "An Eighth Grader Gets Angry"

The Facts of Life continued

Q229. When Mrs. Garrett, the school dietitian, couldn't get a raise and the school lost her pension fund, she quit to open Edna's Edibles, a gourmet food store. What was the name of the place Edna took over?

Family Matters
ABC, 1989–

Q230. Carl and Harriette Winslow reside at 263 Pinehurst Street in Chicago with their children, Edward, Laura, and Judy. Carl was first an officer, then a sergeant with what division of the police department?

Q231. In his youth, Carl was an expert pool player. At the Corner Pocket, where he played pool, he had a nickname. What was it?

Q232. Carl also held a job as a TV traffic reporter on the four o'clock news of what TV station?

Q233. Harriette is the security director at the *Chicago Chronicle*. What job at the paper did she hold prior to acquiring this one?

Q234. Middle child Laura is pretty, fashion conscious, and bright. What is the scent of her favorite perfume?

Q235. Rachel is Harriette's beautiful younger sister and she also lives with the family. When Laura's favorite after-school hangout burned down, Rachel reopened it as a diner called Rachel's Place. What was the original name?

Q236. Steve Urkel met Laura Winslow in kindergarten. She made him eat Playdoh and he has been in love with her ever since. A straight A student, Steve has a stay-away fund (his relatives send him money so he will not visit them), and Laura too, wants nothing to do with him. In a home economics class the unthinkable happened: he got a C and fainted. What caused Steve to get a C?

A229. Ara's Deli

Family Matters

A230. Metro Division of the Eighth Precinct

A231. "Rack and Roll Winslow"

A232. WNTW, Channel 13

A233. Elevator operator

A234. "Rainbow Cloud"

A235. LeRoy's

A236. He tried to make bread but the yeast didn't rise.

Family Matters continued

Q237. The equipment manager of the golf club at school, Steve boasts about being 98 percent brain and 2 percent brawn. He also has a very unusual favorite snack. What is it?

Family Ties
NBC, 1982–89

Q238. Steven Keaton and Elyse O'Donnell, flower children who met in college in the late 1960s, married after attending Woodstock and set up housekeeping in a commune where their first son, Alex, was born. Alex was the second-choice name; what was the first?

Q239. In college, Steven was president of the south campus aluminum can recycling program. He also wrote a play. What was it called?

Q240. Elyse had always dreamed of becoming a folksinger, but turned her talents to becoming an architect. What was the first structure Elyse designed?

Q24l. Studious Alex P. Keaton, who had a collection of his report cards from nursery school through college, worshipped money and prided himself on being different. At Leland College, Alex had a radio program that mixed blues music with business news. What was the program called?

Q242. Alex majored in economics and accepted a job with what Wall Street firm?

Q243. Mallory, the second-born child, was very pretty and bright in her own way, with dreams of becoming a fashion designer. She had what she called a special gift for this profession. What is it?

Q244. A devout mall-shopper, Mallory attended Grant College, which "is conveniently located near all major highways." She also wrote a column for the *Columbus Shoppers' Guide*. What was it called?

A237. Anchovy paste on a dog biscuit

Family Ties

A238. Moon Muffin

A239. *A Draft Card for Burning*

A240. The Cavanaugh Building in Columbus

A241. "Syncopated Money"

A242. O'Brien, Mathers, and Clark

A243. Being able to tell fabrics apart blindfolded

A244. "Dear Mallory"

Family Ties continued

Q245. While her family disapproved of him, Mallory was crazy in love with grungy-looking Nick Moore, a struggling artist. What was the first painting Nick sold?

Q246. Jennifer was the third child, a member of the Sunshine Girls Club who attended Harding High School. She also had an after-school job at what fast-food store?

Father Knows Best
CBS/NBC/ABC, 1954–62

Q247. Jim and Margaret Anderson lived in the small town of Springfield with their children Betty, Bud, and Kathy. Jim was the all-around problem solver although he claimed "I'm just an ordinary guy who sells insurance." For whom did Jim work?

Q248. Jim and Margaret donated $25 each year to the Children's Home Society, and Margaret was a member of the Women's Club of Springfield. What daily paper did they read?

Q249. Betty was the oldest of the children and the smartest as well as the most sensitive. When something troubled Betty, she retreated to the edge of a brook in Sycamore Grove Park to sort things out. What did she call this spot?

Flying Blind
Fox, 1992–93

Q250. Alicia and Neal were lovers, two opposites who found an attraction to each other. At what restaurant in New York City did they meet?

Q251. The sexy Alicia, who worked as a model, once was an actress and became famous for what horror film produced by Specter Films?

A245.   "Woman With a Half-Eaten Hamburger"

A246.   Chicken Heaven

Father Knows Best

A247.   The General Insurance Company

A248.   The *Springfield Star News*

A249.   Her Secret Thinking Place

Flying Blind

A250.   The Apollo

A251.   *Bride of the Marsh Monster*

Flying Blind continued

Q252. *Beverly Hills, 9021-Dead* and *Massacre at Cleavage Farm* were two other films produced by Specter, the low-budget movie company that employed Neal. Name at least one other film that was mentioned which the company produced.

The Fresh Prince of Bel Air
NBC, 1990–

Q253. Will Smith is the "Fresh Prince" of the title, a troubled West Philly teenager who is sent to live with rich relatives, Philip and Vivian Banks in Bel Air in an attempt to straighten him out. Now enrolled in the prestigious Bel Air Academy, Will earns extra spending money by working as a waiter in what restaurant?

Q254. As a kid Philip lived on a farm in Nebraska and won the Young Farmers of America Pig Passing Contest four years in a row. What was the name of his pet pig?

Q255. Vivian is a professor who substitutes at various schools. She loves gourmet meals and is nuts about one particular flavor of ice cream. What is it?

Q256. Twenty-one-year-old Hilary is Philip and Vivian's oldest child. She is beautiful and very feminine and has her hair done at what parlor?

Q257. When Hilary was nine, she took up the violin but gave it up "because it irritated my chin." She next took up ballet, but soon gave that up. Why?

Q258. Carlton, the middle child, hopes to follow in his father's footsteps and become a lawyer. He is a member of the school's poetry and glee clubs and had his first crush on what TV character?

A252. *The Revenge of the Mutant Ozone Mermaids* and *Frosty the Maniac*

The Fresh Prince of Bel Air

A253. The Brawny Deep

A254. Melvin

A255. Vanilla Swiss Almond

A256. Black Beauty

A257. "Because I thought I would get feet like Fred Flintstone."

A258. Tootie (from *The Facts of Life*)

Full House
ABC, 1987–

Q259. Friday is "Mop the floors till you drop day" at the Tanner house in San Francisco. Danny Tanner, a widower with three daughters (D.J., Stephanie, and Michelle), now cohosts *Wake Up, San Francisco* with Rebecca Donaldson on Channel 8. What TV job did Danny work at before this show?

Q260. Danny is a neat freak who attributes his excessive neatness to his fifth birthday, when his mother gave him a set of vacuum cleaner attachments and called him her "special helper." At this same time Danny also had a "friend" he made from a washcloth. What did he name it?

Q261. D.J. is the oldest of the Tanner girls. She loves to shop at the mall "and spend hours in the bathroom." As a kid she had a favorite pillow. What did she call it?

Q262. D.J. wears "Passion Plum" eye shadow and held a job as "The Happy Helper" for what mall photographer?

Q263. Middle child Stephanie, whose catchphrase is "How rude," carries a Jetsons lunch box to school and has a favorite plush bear. What does she call the bear?

Q264. Danny, the coach of Stephanie's Little League Team, the Giants, is proud of his daughter for the curve ball she can throw. What does he call it?

Q265. Michelle is the baby of the family. "You got it, dude!" is her favorite expression; *The Little Mermaid* is her favorite movie, and she enjoys eating what cereal for breakfast?

Q266. Danny's brother-in-law, Jesse, and his best friend, Joey, help Danny in raising the girls. Jesse and Joey are business partners and run what commercial jingle-writing company?

Q267. Jesse, who idolizes Elvis Presley, has a band, Jesse and the Rippers. In high school Jesse was also part of another group. What was its name?

Full House

A259. Sportscaster on *Newsbeat*

A260. Terry the talking washcloth

A261. Pillow Person

A262. Tot Shots

A263. Mr. Bear

A264. The Tanner Twister

A265. Honey Coated Fiber Bears

A266. J.J. Creative Services (later, Double J Creative Services)

A267. Discipline Problem

Full House continued

Q268. Joey is also a talented stand-up comic who got a big break when he was signed to do a TV pilot with Annette Funicello and Frankie Avalon. What was the title of the pilot?

Q269. Pretty Kimmy Gibler is D.J.'s best friend. "People say I look like Julia Roberts. I wish I was Madonna. She's rich." Kimmy cuts home economics classes ("'cause I'm gonna marry a doctor and hire a maid") and writes what column for the school newspaper?

The George Burns and Gracie Allen Show
CBS, 1950–58

Q270. "If it weren't for Gracie's antics," George Burns said, "I'd be selling ties." George and Gracie met in vaudeville, and when they first dated, he gave her flowers. Gracie saved those flowers by pressing them between the pages of what book?

Q271. "My Life With George Burns" was an article Gracie wrote for a magazine in 1952. She had to type it twice (she tried using carbon paper "but it's black and you can't see what you type on it"). In what magazine did the article appear?

Q272. George and Gracie's neighbors were Harry and Blanche Morton. Harry, a C.P.A., was very fussy and would drink only one kind of alcoholic beverage. What was it?

The Ghost and Mrs. Muir
NBC/ABC, 1968–70

Q273. Gull Cottage, in the New England town of Schooner Bay, was haunted by the ghost of a sea captain named Daniel Gregg, and went unoccupied for many years before Carolyn Muir and her children, Candy and Jonathan, moved in—despite its "curse." Though balking at having the Muirs live in his house, the Captain tolerated them. When Captain Gregg originally built the house in the 1800s, what plans did he have for it?

A268. *Surf's Up*

A269. "Madame Kimmy's Horoscope."

The George Burns and Gracie Allen Show

A270. *A Report on the Sheep Herding Industry*

A271. *Look*

A272. Blackberry cordial

The Ghost and Mrs. Muir

A273. A home for retired sailors

The Ghost and Mrs. Muir continued

Q274. Now that Carolyn had made the captain's cabin (Daniel's bedroom) hers, he only had one place of refuge left in the house. What room was it (Daniel called it "the wheel house")?

Q275. "Blast" and "Blasted" were the captain's favorite expressions. He has also made one part of the house his bridge (where he stood watch each night). Where was the captain's bridge?

Q276. Martha, the Muirs' housekeeper, disliked Captain Gregg even though she was unaware of his ghostly presence. What "term of endearment" did Martha use for the captain?

Gidget
ABC, 1965–66

Q277. Frances Lawrence, nicknamed "Gidget"—a girl who is not tall or a midget: a Gidget—lived in Santa Monica with her widowed father, Russ, an English professor. Her passion was surfing and she was in love with a surfer named Moondoggie. When Gidget was on the phone with her friends, and her sister (Anne) or father walked into the room, she had slang terms to warn the person she was talking to. Name either term.

Q278. When the rock band fad hit Santa Monica, Gidget formed a group, The Young People. When she found them too clean-cut, she radically changed their appearance and renamed them. What did she call them?

A274.   The attic

A275.   On the porch above Carolyn's room

A276.   "The Old Barnacle"

Gidget

A277.   "Parentville" and "Sisterville"

A278.   Gidget and the Gorries

Gilligan's Island
CBS, 1964–67

Q279. The uncharted island about three hundred miles south-east of Hawaii was home to seven castaways when their ship was destroyed in a surprise storm. Among them was millionaire Thurston Howell III, called "The Wolf of Wall Street" and head of Howell Industries, who tried to make the best of a primitive lifestyle and still enjoy some past pleasures like playing polo. What was the name of the practice polo pony the Professor made for him out of bamboo?

Q280. Thurston attended SMU (Super Millionaires University) and was very insistent about the temperature of his bath water. What did it have to be?

Q281. Ginger was a gorgeous movie star who broke into show business in a mind-reading act with Merlin the Mind Reader. She later won a beauty contest. What was she voted?

Q282. *Sing a Song of Sing Sing, San Quentin Blues*, and *Mohawk Over the Moon* were three of the five movies Ginger made. Name one of the other two.

Q283. The Professor was a high school science teacher whose knowledge made life as comfortable as possible on the island. After his first week there, he made what he considered a fantastic discovery. What was it?

Good Times
CBS, 1974–79

Q284. The Evans Family lived in Apartment 17C of the Cabrini Housing Project in Chicago. What was their monthly rent?

Q285. Florida, the mother, had to take a job to support the family after her husband, James, was killed in a car accident after the second TV season. For whom did Florida work?

Gilligan's Island

A279.   Bruce

A280.   79 degrees

A281.   "Miss Hourglass" ("They said I had all the sand in the right places.")

A282.   "The Rain Dancers of Rango Rango" or "Belly Dancers From Bali Bali"

A283.   Five different mutations of ragweed

Good Times

A284. $104

A285.   Roadway Bus Company

Good Times *continued*

Q286. Resourceful, bop-talking J.J. was the oldest child and a hopeful artist. Before working for a greeting card company, J.J. held a job at what fast-food place?

Q287. "Buffalo Butt" was the name J.J. and neighbor Willona called Nathan Bookman, the building's overweight janitor. Of what fraternity was Nathan a member?

Green Acres
CBS, 1965–71

Q288. Lisa and Oliver Douglas traded in their life of luxury on Park Avenue to become farmers in the small town of Hooterville. Their new digs, a rather decrepit house, was actually a local landmark—the birthplace of "the founder of the great state of Hooterville." Who founded Hooterville?

Q289. Probably the only farmer in the world who did his chores wearing a suit and tie, Oliver was also most likely the only one to plow his fields with an ancient, broken-down tractor. What make of tractor did Oliver own?

Q290. Handyman Eb Dawson constantly called Oliver "Dad" even though they were not related. Eb sort of came with the farm and had a poster of his hero on his bedroom wall. What Western movie star was Eb's hero?

Q291. Although he was a pig, his official name was Arnold Ziffel. Arnold attended third grade, liked lime soda, and played cricket. He also had a favorite TV show. What was it?

Growing Pains
ABC, 1988–92

Q292. Jason and Maggie Seaver, a professional couple with four children (Mike, Carol, Ben and Chrissy), lived in Huntington, New York. The Seavers' garbage was picked up on Tuesdays and Fridays by whom?

A286.   Chicken Shack

A287.   The Jolly Janitors Club

Green Acres

A288.   Rutherford B. Skrugg

A289.   Hoyt-Clagwell

A290.   Hoot Gibson

A291.   *The CBS Evening News With Walter Cronkite*

Growing Pains

A292.   Municipal Removal Service

Growing Pains continued

Q293. Jason was a psychologist who left his job at a hospital to open a private practice from his home. Where did Jason initially work?

Q294. Maggie majored in journalism and for two years was a researcher for *Newsweek* magazine before giving up her career to raise a family. When Jason set up his practice at home, Maggie returned to work. For what paper did she become a reporter?

Q295. Oldest child Mike was the number-one problem student at school, and it seemed highly unlikely that he would become a teacher, but he did. Prior to this he was an aspiring actor. On what TV show did Mike make his acting debut?

Q296. Carol, the older daughter, attended Dewey High School and Columbia University. She was studying law and took what subway train to get to school?

Q297. Benjamin Hubert Humphrey Seaver was the third born. He attended Wendell Willkie Elementary School and had an imaginary friend. What was the friend's name?

Q298. Chrissy, the youngest, was born at 12:30 A.M. and weighed eight pounds four ounces. Her favorite story was "Mr. Mouse," and she had several plush toys—a whale, a bear, and a pig. She called the pig "Papa Pig." What did she call the whale and bear?

Happy Days

ABC, 1974–84

Q299. Life in the 1950s was depicted through the experiences of the Cunningham family: parents Howard and Marion and their children Richie and Joanie. Howard owned the Cunningham Hardware Store. What service did he offer?

Q300. When Howard first went into a certain hardware store and saw the shelves lined with goods, he was hooked. He became a stockboy and by 1946 he owned the place. From what supplier did Howard get his goods?

A293.   Long Island General Hospital

A294.   *Long Island Daily Herald*

A295.   *New York Heat*

A296.   The Number One I.R.T.

A297.   Pirate Pete

A298.   The whale was Mr. Blow Hole; the bear was Bertha Big Jeans

Happy Days

A299.   Free paint color-mixing

A300.   Ernie's Hardware Store

Happy Days *continued*

Q301. Richie was called "Freckles" as a kid (age nine) and was said to resemble Howdy Doody. Meat loaf was his favorite dinner, but what was his favorite breakfast?

Q302. It had the license plate number F-7193 and it was Richie's first car, a 1952 Ford. What did he call the car?

Q303. Joanie, Richie's sister, was fondly called "Shortcake" and "Pumpkin." She was a member of the Junior Chipmunks Scout Troop and attended Jefferson High School. As anyone knows who watched the show, Howard was always talking about something that became Joanie's first word as a baby. What was her first word?

Q304. While Richie's favorite meal was meat loaf, Joanie preferred something totally different. What was it?

Q305. Arthur Herbert Fonzarelli, better known as "The Fonz" or "Fonzie," was the cool, leather-jacketed high school dropout admired by everyone. The Fonz had a bathrobe that said "Sweetums" ("Hey, it was a gift from a girl") and he used what brand of after-shave lotion?

Q306. While Fonzie seemed to have almost everything, including any girl he wanted, he was plagued by "The Fonzarelli Curse." What was it?

Q307. Boy-crazy Jenny Piccolo, Joanie's best friend, called herself "the object of mad desire." Jenny was not as busty as she would have liked to be. What did she order to make herself "more of a sexpot than I already am?"

Q308. Arnold's Drive-In was the famous after-school hangout. Fonzie's "offices" were in the "Guy's Room," and there was a soda machine near the front door. What brand did it dispense?

A301. Blueberry pancakes and fresh-squeezed orange juice

A302. The Love Bandit

A303. "Hardware"

A304. Baked macaroni and apple sauce

A305. Mr. Musk

A306. "When I'm asked to be best man at a wedding, disaster happens."

A307. The Ajax Bust Developer

A308. Spring Time Cola

Hazel
NBC/CBS, 1961–66

Q309. "Who's the gal who's everybody's pal, it's Hazel; she's the one who can make the sun begin to glow..." Thus goes the theme to this now classic TV series. Hazel was the maid to the Baxters: George, Dorothy, and son, Harold. She was the all-around problem solver and a member of what society of maids?

Q310. Hazel's insurance policy covered her back when she bowled, and she was famous for her fudge brownies. She also owned eleven shares of stock in what company?

Q311. George said that "Hazel will never tell a lie; she has George Washington heroics." He also declared that Hazel was the only person who knew the true meaning of Christmas. Why?

Q312. Hazel served breakfast at seven o'clock, lunch at 12:15, and dinner at 6:30. She took time off to attend mass on Sunday and had one day a week off. What day was it?

Q313. George, a lawyer, attended Dartmouth, was a member of the board of regents of the university law school, and began practicing in 1949. Name the firm for which George worked (and was a partner).

Q314. George was particularly fond of Hazel's fudge brownies. What did he call them?

Q315. Dorothy, a free-lance interior decorator, bought her dresses at Monteque's Boutique. Where did she buy her lingerie?

Q316. Herbert and Harriet Johnson were the Baxters' elderly neighbors and George's clients. Herbert was a retired investor who cornered the market on whale bones. How many whale bones did he have?

Q317. In the last-season episodes, Hazel became the maid to George's younger brother, Steve, his wife, Barbara, and their daughter, Susie. Hazel and Barbara attempted to make money by marketing a chili sauce created by Hazel. What did they call the product?

Hazel

A309.   The Sunshine Girls

A310.   The Davidson Vacuum Cleaner Company

A311.   She makes her own presents.

A312.   Thursday

A313.   Butterworth, Hatch, Noll, and Baxter

A314.   Hazel's Peachy Keen Pecan Brownies

A315.   Blackstone's Department Store

A316.   427 tons

A317.   Aunt Hazel's Chili Sauce

Head of the Class
ABC, 1986–91

Q318. Before becoming a teacher at Fillmore High School, Charlie Moore was an actor who appeared in plays by Chekhov and Ibsen and directed the Off-Broadway play *The Little Shop of Horrors*. He also was in an Off-Broadway production of *Hair* and considered it to be his most embarrassing moment. Why?

Q319. Before leaving Fillmore to star in the road production of *Death of a Salesman*, Charlie worked as the "King of Discount Appliances" for what company?

Q320. Billy MacGregor replaced Charlie as the history teacher for the I.H.P. (Individual Honors Program) students. Billy was from Scotland and took a second job shortly after joining the Fillmore staff. Where was it?

Q321. Bernadette Meara, the assistant principal, was born in North Carolina and came to New York in 1974 for the job. She enjoyed the Christmas holidays, but when she was seven, she experienced the saddest Christmas of her life. What happened?

Q322. Simone was the prettiest girl in the Honors Program. Her specialty was English and she had a romantic vision of life. She also was a member of the chess club, but lost all her femininity in the class. Why?

Q323. Wealthy Darlene believed she was very attractive to men ("I represent the physical and intellectual ideals men want"). She was also a descendant of which historically famous black woman?

Q324. Arvid had a perfect attendance record. Nothing stopped him—not blizzards, hurricanes, subway strikes, or illness. How many days of school had Arvid logged by October 1990?

Q325. Arvid played triangle in the school orchestra, was the lunchroom monitor, and admired writer Carl Sagan. When he got upset, he opened his wallet and talked to a picture of what famous person?

Head of the Class

A318.   He did the nude scene in the wrong act.

A319.   Veemer Appliances

A320.   The Mother Hubbard Day Care Center

A321.   She didn't get a Susie Q Easy Bake Oven.

A322.   The teacher called her "Mister."

A323.   Sally Hemmings, by whom Thomas Jefferson had children.

A324.   2,252

A325.   Albert Einstein

Head of the Class continued

Q326. Dennis was skilled in chemistry and physics, but was also the practical-joke player among his classmates. His antics got him sent to the principal's office so many times that he lost count. While waiting to be scolded, what did he do?

Q327. The I.H.P. classes were held in Room 19, where there was a Rand-McNally map on the wall and two computers. What did the kids call the computers?

Home Improvement
ABC, 1991–

Q328. Tim Taylor is the host of a comical home improvement show in Detroit. His wife, Jill, complains most often that he leaves the cap off the toothpaste tube. On the show, Tim is assisted by Al, who also carps about the things Tim forgets to do, like leaving the cap off what?

Q329. While Tim may be boss of his garage workshop, Jill is the boss of the kitchen. She has two sponges and what specific rules for them?

Q330. Tim is obsessed with tools, especially those made by the show's sponsor, Binford Tools, and likes to shop for them. Where is he considered a valued customer?

The Honeymooners
CBS, 1955–56

Q331. He promised Alice the moon, but he was rarely able to provide any luxuries for her. Ralph Kramden was a bus driver and earned $60 a week, but in 1955 it never seemed enough, and he ventured into many money-making schemes that all failed. He tried to market the Handy Housewife Helper on TV (as "The Chef of the Future") and he attempted low-cal pizza and glow-in-the-dark wallpaper (to cut down on electric bills). But he was most famous for investing in something. What was it?

A326. Stared at a picture of George Washington that is on the wall.

A327. Fred and Wilma

Home Improvement

A328. The epoxy glue tube

A329. The blue sponge is for the sink; the green sponge is for the counter

A330. Damon's Hardware Store

The Honeymooners

A331. A uranium mine in Asbury Park

The Honeymooners *continued*

Q332. Ralph and Alice had few electrical appliances, and their typical gas bill was thirty-nine cents a month. Still, to supplement their income, Alice took a job as a jelly donut stuffer at what bakery?

Q333. Edward L. Norton and his wife, Trixie, were the Kramdens' upstairs neighbors. Ed majored in arithmetic at vocational school and now works in sewers. As a kid he had a dog named Lulu and mentioned that the "L" in his name stood for what?

Q334. Ed and Ralph were members of the Raccoon Lodge and also bowled on the same team. What was the team's name?

Q335. To become a lodge member, one had to have a public school diploma, be a resident of the United States for at least six months, and pay a $1.50 initiation fee. The most expensive aspect of being a member was the cost of the uniform. How much was it?

I Love Lucy
CBS, 1951–57

Q336. Fred and Ethel Mertz were the owners of the Manhattan brownstone that was home to bandleader Ricky Ricardo and his scatterbrained wife, Lucy. The Ricardos lived in Apartment 3B and paid how much a month rent?

Q337. Lucy was born in Jamestown, New York. When she attended grade school what did the kids call her?

Q338. At Jamestown High, Lucy was Juliet in the school's production of *Romeo and Juliet* and was a member of the band. She played the saxophone but only learned one song. What was it?

Q339. Perhaps one of the most famous episodes in the series was the one in which Lucy becomes intoxicated while doing a commercial for Vitameatavegamin, a vitamin product with a 32 percent alcohol content. But what program was the commercial for?

A332. Krausmeyer's

A333. Lilywhite (his mother's maiden name)

A334. The Hurricanes

A335. $35

I Love Lucy

A336. $125

A337. "Bird Legs"

A338. "Glow Worm"

A339. *Your Saturday Night Variety Show*

I Love Lucy continued

Q340. Lucy's goal was to break into show business despite Ricky's objections. While it was not a glitzy dance number in one of Ricky's shows, "Breakfast with Lucy and Ricky" made Lucy a TV star when she cohosted it. What company sponsored the show?

Q341. Lucy and Ricky became the parents of Little Ricky in 1953. The youngster had a number of pets, including a dog, two fish, two parakeets, two turtles, and a frog. Little Ricky called the frog Hopalong and the dog Fred. What were the names of either the fish or parakeets?

Q342. Ricky's most annoying habit, according to Lucy, was tapping his fingers. What did Ricky say was Lucy's most annoying habit?

Q343. Ethel claimed that Fred's habit of jingling his keys was most annoying to her, but what did Fred say Ethel's most annoying habit was?

I Married Joan
NBC, 1952–55

Q344. Joan Stevens called herself "a real goof; a girl who is guaranteed to foul things up." Married to Judge Bradley Stevens, Joan tried hard to be a good housewife and was good at maneuvering the household funds to balance the budget. She couldn't, though, resist shopping for bargains. What did the salesmen call her?

Q345. A member of the Women's Welfare League, Joan considered herself to be very popular. She was a Guy Lombardo fan and loved TV soap operas. What was the title of her favorite one?

Q346. Brad called Joan "Lover" and liked to hear the words "Dinner is ready." What was his favorite meal?

Q347. A domestic relations judge, Brad enjoyed two hobbies. One was hunting. What was the other one?

A340.   Phipps Drug Store

A341.   Alice and Phil (parakeets); Mildred and Charles (fish)

A342.   Hitting the spoon against the side of a cup while stirring coffee.

A343.   "Chewing like a cow."

I Married Joan

A344.   "One of those yo-yo dames."

A345.   *Two Hearts Against the World*

A346.   Pot roast

A347.   Stamp collecting

The Jack Benny Program
CBS/NBC, 1950–65

Q348. He had been thirty-nine for so long that Jack Benny had forgotten how old he really was. He also claimed that his writers were responsible for the image people had of him as being cheap. Jack had a vault in his basement, but he also had funds in the bank, and while he rarely withdrew money from the bank, he loved to visit it. What happened when Jack went to the bank?

Q349. Jack had a laundry business on the side and enjoyed attending parties, so much so that he was listed in the yellow pages. What did his listing say?

Q350. While Jack Benny actually could play the violin, he faked being a terrible violinist on the air. He also thought of himself as a songwriter. Name the awful song he composed.

Q351. Real-life wife Mary Livingstone was Jack's radio and TV girlfriend, a salesgirl at the May Company. Jack sometimes treated Mary to dinner (if he could find a cheap enough restaurant) and did take her on dates. However, what was Jack's idea of seeing a movie with Mary?

Just the Ten of Us
ABC, 1988–90

Q352. The Lubbocks were a family of ten residing in Eureka, California. Graham and Elizabeth were the parents, and their children were Marie, Wendy, Cindy, Connie, Sherry, J.R., and infant twins Michelle and Harvey. Graham was the football coach at St. Augie's. What was the name of the team?

Q353. Marie, Wendy, Connie, and Cindy formed a singing group called the Lubbock Babes. A big hit in Eureka, the girls performed regularly at what local eatery?

Q354. Seventeen-year-old Wendy was the prettiest of the girls. She was boy-crazy and wore a size 7½ shoe and a size 5 dress. Name one of the two shades of lipstick she wore.

The Jack Benny Program

A348.   He caused a run on it.

A349.   "Available for Parties"

A350.   "When You Say I Beg Your Pardon, Then I'll Come Back to You"

A351.   Going over to her house because the TV screen was bigger.

Just the Ten of Us

A352.   The Hippos

A353.   Danny's Pizza Parlor

A354.   "Dawn at His Place" or "Midnight Passion"

Just the Ten of Us continued

Q355. Cindy was the not-too-bright Lubbock Babe. She was sixteen, had a slight weight problem, and her middle name was Anne. However, it was only late in the series that Cindy realized Anne was her middle name. What did she believe her middle name was?

Q356. Connie, the most intelligent of the children, was fifteen and also the most sensitive. She hoped to become a writer, but her first job was sweeping up animal entrails at what slaughterhouse?

Kate and Allie
CBS, 1984–88

Q357. We all know them as Kate and Allie, single mothers who shared a Manhattan apartment to save on expenses. They first met as kids at the orthodontist and each character had a full name. What were those names?

Q358. Kate worked while Allie cared for her children, Jennie and Chip, and Kate's daughter, Emma. For what company did Kate work, and at what school did Allie take night classes?

Q359. Whether it was Christmas or a birthday, Kate and Allie always exchanged the same gifts. Allie gave Kate a purse. What did Kate give Allie?

Q360. In 1988 Allie married Bob Barsky, a famous football player turned TV sportscaster. For what station did Bob work?

Laverne and Shirley
ABC, 1976–83

Q361. Laverne DeFazio and Shirley Feeney, blue-collar friends who shared an apartment in Milwaukee during the 1960s, shopped at Slotnick's Supermarket, and worked in the bottle-capping division of the Shotz Brewery. When the girls served a hitch in the army, Shirley wrote of their experiences under what pen name?

A355.　Diane

A356.　MacGregor's

Kate and Allie

A357.　Kate was Katherine Elizabeth Ann McArdle; Allie was
　　　　Allison Julie Charlotte Adams Lowell.

A358.　Kate worked for the Sloane Travel Agency; Allie attended
　　　　Washington Square College.

A359.　A sweater

A360.　WNTD, Channel 10

Laverne and Shirley

A361.　S. Wilhelmina Feeney

Laverne and Shirley continued

Q362. Laverne suffered from claustrophobia, and milk and Pepsi was her favorite drink. What was her favorite sandwich?

Q363. Shirley had a plush cat named Boo Boo Kitty and was famous for the Shirley Feeney Scarf Dance. What was the one food Shirley would not order with extra barbecue sauce ("It's messy and gets under my nails")?

Q364. Lenny and Squiggy were Laverne and Shirley's friends, although they didn't like that to be known by too many people. Lenny enjoyed horror movies and sports, but as a kid he had only what one "toy" to play with?

Q365. Squiggy was most proud of his moth collection and had been blessed with the family birthmark. What was it?

Q366. When the series switched locales to California, Lenny and Squiggy became ice cream vendors and talent agents. To meet young starlets they wrote a horror movie. What was it called?

Leave It to Beaver
CBS/ABC, 1957–62

Q367. The Cleavers—Ward and June and young sons Wally and Beaver—lived at 211 Pine Street in the town of Mayfield. Ward, who grew up on Shaker Avenue and was an engineer with the Seabees during World War II, enjoyed fishing and reading the daily newspaper. What was the paper's name?

Q368. Wally was a three-letter man at Mayfield High School whose best time as a member of the swimming team was 53.2 seconds. He also played varsity football and wore what brand of after-shave lotion?

Q369. Younger brother Beaver had the real first name of Theodore. Whom was Theodore named after?

A362.   Peanut butter and sauerkraut on raisin bread

A363.   Chicken

A364.   Sauerkraut

A365.   A red blotch shaped like Abraham Lincoln.

A366.   *Blood Orgy of the Amazon*

Leave It to Beaver

A367.   *The Mayfield Press*

A368.   Arabian Knights

A369.   June's Aunt Martha's brother

Leave It to Beaver continued

Q370. Beaver wasn't much for mushy stuff and liked to "mess around with junk." He hated girls but loved fishing. Where did he fish?

Q371. Wally's friend, Eddie Haskell, was overly polite to adults but mean to everybody else, especially Beaver, whom he called "Squirt." He also used three nicknames for Wally. Name two of them.

Q372. The wisecracking Eddie was also the first of Wally's buddies to get a credit card. To show off, he also misused it. What outfit issued Eddie a card?

Q373. Ward's occupation was never revealed, although it appeared he may have been an accountant. At any rate, he worked for Fred Rutherford. What did Fred call Ward?

Love and War
CBS, 1992–

Q374. The Blue Shamrock, a Manhattan bar owned by Wally Porter, was frequented by Jack Stein, Mary Margaret Tynan, and Ray Litvak. Before purchasing the place Wally owned a classy uptown restaurant on East 72nd Street. What was it called?

Q375. Wally is a renowned gourmet cook. She can serve twelve dinners in twenty-one minutes and debone a chicken in how many seconds?

Q376. Kip Zakaris is Wally's ex-husband, an impossibly vain actor who appeared Off-Broadway in *West Side Story* (playing Jet #2); on TV's *Lou Grant* (a deranged typesetter); and in what often mentioned pilot "about a meat inspector who drives a Ferrari"?

Q377. Newspaper columnist Jack Stein, Wally's romantic interest, won an award for a story on illiteracy. What is the name of his column?

A370. Miller's Lake

A371. "Sam," "Gertrude," or "Ellwood"

A372. Universal Gas and Oil Company

A373. "Lord of the Manor"

Love and War

A374. The Chez Wally Restaurant

A375. Twenty

A376. "Turf and Surf"

A377. "The Steinway"

Love That Bob
NBC/CBS, 1955–59

Q378. Bob Collins was a swinging young bachelor who owned a photography studio in Hollywood. A confirmed bachelor, he needed time to find the right girl—"no matter how many girls I have to date to find her." Bob simply could not resist a beautiful woman and wore what cologne that drove them crazy?

Q379. Bob may have worked long hours but he rarely complained when it came to photographing beautiful models. However, he insisted that his swimsuit models could not have a waist larger than what size?

Q380. "The Casanova of the camera," as his sister Margaret called him, found which month of the year the most difficult in which to stay single?

Q381. Some of the most beautiful women in movies appeared on *Love That Bob*, including blond Joi Lansing as Shirley Swanson, a model who was determined to marry Bob. She took no chances, and even her perfume spelled trouble for him. What perfume did Shirley wear?

Mad About You
NBC, 1992–

Q382. Paul and Jamie are the married couple mad about each other. They live in Manhattan and have a dog named Murray. Paul, born in New York City and a graduate of NYU Film School, now runs his own documentary film company. What does he call it?

Q383. Jamie was born in Connecticut and attended Yale University. She likes to be liked by people, and when she feels someone she would like to know doesn't like her, she goes to extremes—as in high school when she did something to impress a boy. Because of what she did, she got a reputation. What was she called?

Love That Bob

A378.   Moustache

A379.   23 inches

A380.   June—when girls are the most marriage-minded.

A381.   "Bachelor's Doom"

Mad About You

A382.   Buchman Films

A383.   "The Stemple sister who showed a boy her boobs to be liked."

Madame's Place
Syndicated, 1982–83

Q384. Madame, the hand puppet of Wayland Flowers, was the host of *Madame's Place*, a late night talk show that broadcast from her Beverly Hills mansion. She began her career as a comedienne in dingy clubs but hit the big time in movies, and starred with Clint Eastwood in what mythical movie of which she was most proud?

Q385. Madame read the *Enquiring Star* and was a member of the Fetish of the Month Club. What brand of body rubbing oil did she order?

Q386. Sara Joy Pitts was Madame's ultrasexy niece, coming to Hollywood from Georgia to be an actress "like my auntie Madame." Not-too-bright Sara Joy watched what favorite TV soap opera with the sound off "because it's so sad and it makes me cry"?

Q387. A former "two-bit band singer," Lynn LaVecque went on to host a show that is aired opposite *Madame's Place*. What was the name of Lynn's show that was costing Madame viewers.

Major Dad
CBS, 1989–93

Q388. John MacGillis was a tough marine who married a widow (Polly) with three daughters (Elizabeth, Robin, and Casey). He was born in Mississippi, where his grandfather taught him to whittle and where, at the age of seven, he made the biggest mistake of his life. What was it?

Q389. John was originally stationed in Oceanside, California, then in Furlough, Virginia, where he was the aide to Gen. Marcus Craig. What was the nickname for the job John held?

Q390. In California, Polly was a reporter for the *Oceanside Chronicle*. For what paper did she work when the family moved to Virginia?

Madame's Place

A384.   *A Woman Named Hey You*

A385.   "Me Tarzan—You Jane"

A386.   *The Young and the Stupid*

A387.   *Naked All-Star Bowling*

Major Dad

A388.   He stole a Zorro wristwatch that cost $7.95.

A389.   "Staff Weenie"

A390.   Writer for the camp newspaper, *The Bulldog*

Major Dad continued

Q391. Teenage Elizabeth was the prettiest of the girls, but was somewhat embarrassed when looking through the family photo album. Why?

Q392. Sister Robin was the tomboy of the family. In California she was a member of the school's basketball team, the Condors. In Virginia she was in the girls' softball league. What was the name of her team?

Q393. Casey, the youngest, had two dolls, a bird, and a teddy bear. Lemon was the name of the bird, and Ruby and Henrietta were the dolls. What did Casey call her teddy bear?

Q394. Alva Lou Bricker, nicknamed "Gunny," was General Craig's administrative chief. She referred to Casey as "Little Cooper," and she herself had a dog. What did she call it?

Q395. When Marcus Craig, the commanding officer of Camp Hollister, got upset, he went to the firing range to shoot off several hundred rounds. He was often upset by his wife who, although never seen, was constantly mentioned. What was her name?

Mama's Family
NBC, 1983–84

Q396. The Harpers were a not-so-typical family living in the mythical Raytown, U.S.A. Thelma "Mama" Harper was the cantankerous head of the family. Her street address was now 1542 Ray Way, but many years ago it had been 10 Decatur Road, at which time it was a brothel. What was the brothel called?

Q397. Mama wore a perfume called "Obsession" and she was a member of the Raytown Community Church League. She was also most secretive about the ingredients in what favorite recipe?

A391. She worried about how her hair looked.

A392. The Hollister Hornets

A393. Mr. Smithers

A394. Elmo

A395. Mimsey

Mama's Family

A396. Ma Beaudien's

A397. Million dollar fudge

Mama's Family continued

Q398. Mama's son, Vinton, was married to Naomi and owned a twenty-five-year collection of *TV Guide*. His favorite watering hole was the Bigger Jigger Bar and he was a member of what fraternity?

Q399. Mama believed Naomi to be the kind of girl mothers fear their sons will marry. Naomi had four previous marriages and worked at what local supermarket?

Q400. Spinster Iola Bolen was Mama's longtime friend. She enjoyed arts and crafts and lived with her own domineering mother. Iola envisioned herself as an actress and performed with what local theater group?

Married... With Children
Fox, 1987–

Q401. Al Bundy is a shoe salesman. As we all know, his wife, Peggy, claims it is the most demeaning, low-paying job there is. What is Al's yearly salary?

Q402. Al has an obsession with "hooters" as he calls them and loves watching such classic films as *Planet of the D Cups* and *Breast Monsters From Venus*. A copy of Al's favorite girlie magazine can be found around the house. What is it?

Q403. The family rarely gets a decent meal because Peggy doesn't shop for food or know that "that big white hot thing in the kitchen" is a stove. For Thanksgiving they have a Bundy turkey (a pizza) and on Labor Day, Bundy Burgers. Exactly what are Bundy Burgers?

Q404. Peggy was born in Wanker County and spends her days watching TV and eating bonbons. She avoids work (around or out of the house) and also refuses to do something that will make Al happy for once in his life. What is it?

A398. Mystic Order of the Cobra Lodge

A399. Food Circus

A400. Peppermint Playhouse Theater Company

Married...with Children

A401. $12,000

A402. *Biggums*

A403. Last year's grease and ashes for this year's burgers

A404. Leave him

Married...With Children continued

Q405. "I was born in February. I'm an aquarium," says Kelly, the mall-shopping Bundy daughter. She had a job as a model representing one of Al's favorite foods (hot dogs wrapped in bread and fried in lard). What title did Kelly hold?

Q406. When needing $400 to enroll in modelling school, Kelly pouted and inveigled money from Al. The course paid off as it got her several jobs, but there was a drawback—she got tension headaches from smiling. Kelly was told, though, she was a natural—a natural at what?

Q407. Kelly calls him "Rat Boy" and "Toad Boy," but Bud, her younger brother, believes he is a ladies' man—despite the laughs from Al and Peggy. When Bud can't get a date, he watches what TV show?

Q408. Bud calls his cowboy pajamas his "love clothes" and Kelly claims that he watches *Star Trek* reruns "to get a glimpse of Klingon cleavage." In an attempt to get girls, Bud has pretended to be a street rapper. What did he call himself?

The Mary Tyler Moore Show
CBS, 1970–77

Q409. Thirty and single, Mary Richards worked as the associate producer of the Channel 12 *Six O'Clock News* in Minneapolis, hired by the show's producer, Lou Grant, because she had spunk "and a nice caboose." While Lou did like Mary's physical features, he hated something about her. What was it?

Q410. Lou played college football and was a distinguished newsman before his job as a news producer. Like clockwork, something came to his office on the fifteenth of each month. What was it?

Q411. Ted Baxter, the station's incompetent newscaster, yearned for a job in New York City with his hero, Walter Cronkite. Despite the grumblings from the news staff, Ted was paid a lot more than they received. What was his yearly salary?

A405. "Miss Weenie Tots"

A406. Leg crossing ("I can do it at will.")

A407. *Dateless Dude Late Night Theater*

A408. Grand Master B.

The Mary Tyler Moore Show

A409. Her parties ("You give rotten parties. I've had some of the worst times of my life at your parties.")

A410. His bar bill

A411. $31,000

The Mary Tyler Moore Show continued

Q412. Rhoda Morganstern, Mary's best friend and upstairs neighbor, moved to Minneapolis when she couldn't find a job or an apartment in New York. A window dresser at Hempell's Department Store, Rhoda had a pet goldfish. What did she call it?

Q413. Shortly after first arriving in Minneapolis, Rhoda went to the zoo, where she was fined $40 for feeding a buffalo. What did she give it?

M*A*S*H
CBS, 1972–83

Q414. Col. Henry Blake was the initial commanding officer of the 4077th M*A*S*H unit in Korea, and loved fishing and clowning around with subordinate officers Hawkeye and Trapper John. From what company did Henry order girlie films for his men?

Q415. Col. Sherman Potter, who replaced Henry as the commanding officer, was born in Missouri and loved horses. Stricter than Henry, he had made the army his career. For doing so, his wife had a nickname for him. What was it?

Q416. Capt. Benjamin Franklin Pierce, better known as "Hawkeye," was drafted, and by defying authority, fought back at the system. He called the unit a cesspool and would not carry a gun. He had a still in his tent and enjoyed reading what magazine?

Q417. Corp. Maxwell Klinger was the unit's resident loon, pretending to be crazy by dressing as a woman to get a Section 8 discharge. While waiting in vain for it to happen, Klinger started a camp newspaper. What did he call it?

Q418. Radar O'Reilly was the company clerk and had the ability to perceive what others think. He also had a number of pets: Moe, Jack, Babette, and Margo (guinea pigs); Fluffy and Bingo (rabbits); and a mouse. What did he call the mouse?

A412. Goldfish

A413. Yogurt

M*A*S*H

A414. Tabasco Films

A415. "Puddin' Head"

A416. *The Joys of Nudity*

A417. "M*A*S*H Notes"

A418. Daisy

*M*A*S*H continued*

Q419. While Hawkeye had his own source for martinis, he also frequented the local watering hole. What was it called?

Mork and Mindy
ABC, 1978–82

Q420. Ork was a planet with three moons whose inhabitants resembled humans but evolved from the chicken. How far from Earth was Ork?

Q421. Orson, a planet leader, assigned Mork to be an Earth Observer and to report to him on Earth activities. What were Mork's telepathic reports to Orson called?

Q422. Mork took up residence with an Earth girl named Mindy McConnell in Boulder, Colorado. Mindy first worked in her father's music store, then as a newscaster at what TV station?

Q423. After Mork and Mindy married (1981), Mork laid an egg that hatched and produced an adult male son they named Mearth (Orkan children are born old and grow younger with time). Mearth attended Ork Prep School one day a month via the Orkan school bus. What was this bus?

Q424. Exidor was the local loon, a fanatic who believed in taking up causes; unfortunately, he did it in all the wrong ways. Brutus was Exidor's invisible dog, but what was the name of his invisible aide?

Mr. Belvedere
ABC, 1985–90

Q425. Lynn Belvedere had appeared on the cover of *World Focus* magazine, had climbed Mount Everest, and had even won the Pillsbury Bake-Off. He had served royalty but now worked as the housekeeper to the Owens, a chaotic family of five in Pittsburgh. At the end of each episode Lynn was seen writing his day's activities in his diary. Name the book he planned to turn his diary into.

A419. Rosie's Bar

Mork and Mindy

A420. 200 million miles

A421. The Scorpio Reports

A422. KTNS, Channel 31

A423. The 828 Transport Beam

A424. Pepe

Mr. Belvedere

A425. *An American Journal: The Suburban Years*

Mr. Belvedere continued

Q426. The Owens family consisted of parents George and Marsha and children Kevin, Heather, and Wesley. George originally hosted "Sports Page" on an AM radio station and he later became the sportscaster for what program on Channel 8?

Q427. Marsha was originally a law student and passed the bar in 1987. With what company did she find work?

Q428. Kevin was the oldest of the children. He attended Van Buren High School and worked part time after school at what fast food store?

Q429. In the middle was Heather, popular at school and with a girlfriend named Angela. Angela was a bit kooky, "and being blonde and pretty are about all Angela has going for her," said Heather. Angela couldn't remember Mr. Belvedere's name (she called him, for example, "Mr. Bell Bottoms" or "Mr. Belly Buster"). What did Angela collect?

Q430. Wesley, the youngest and most mischievous of the Owens children, was a member of the Colts Little League Team and had two pets: a dog and a snake. The dog was Spot; what was the snake's name?

The Munsters
CBS, 1964–66

Q431. The run-down house at 1313 Mockingbird Lane was the residence of the Munster family—parents Herman and Lily, son Eddie, niece Marilyn, and Lily's father, Grandpa. Herman, who resembled Frankenstein, was 150 years old and a gravedigger for Gateman, Goodbury, and Graves. Herman "attended" medical school for six years in several jars. What was the name of the school?

Q432. Herman was over seven feet tall, weighed three spins on the bathroom scale, had a ham radio, and wrote poetry for the company magazine, which published his first poem, "Going Out to Pasture." What was the magazine called?

A426. "Metro News"

A427. The Legal Hut

A428. Mr. Cluck's Fried Chicken

A429. Hangers

A430. Captain Nemo

The Munsters

A431. The Heidelberg School of Medicine

A432. *The Mortician's Monthly*

The Munsters *continued*

Q433. When Herman had a medical exam, the following was revealed: heartbeat none; pulse 15; blood pressure minus three; and what body temperature?

Q434. Lily's maiden name was Dracula. She was 304 years old and her favorite food was bat milk yogurt. Lily did work for what pet charity?

Q435. Grandpa, Lily's father, was an admitted mad scientist, with a lab in the dungeon beneath the Munster Mansion. His favorite TV show was *My Three Sons*. He also had a transistorized divining rod that rarely worked because it picked up the reruns of what old television series?

Q436. The family pet was Spot, a fire-breathing dragon Grandpa found while digging up the backyard. What brand of dog food did Lily feed Spot?

The Munsters Today
Syndicated, 1988–91

Q437. This update of the 1964–66 series *The Munsters* kept most of the aspects of the original show although some changes were made. Herman was now said to be over three hundred years old and worked for Mr. Graves (not Mr. Gateman). As in the original series, Herman was made from a number of different parts, including the muscles of Count Schwarzenegger, the right arm of Igor Johnson (a pickpocket), and the nose of Gregory Fabrock. Who was Gregory Fabrock?

Q438. When Herman felt that the time had come to open his own funeral parlor, he quit his day job and purchased a bankrupt donut shop. What did he call his business?

Q439. Lily was now 324 years old and has been married to Herman for 299 years. Where did Lily work before they wed?

A433.   62.8 degrees

A434.   Bundles for Transylvania

A435.   *My Little Margie*

A436.   Doggie's Din Din

The Munsters Today

A437.   The village idiot

A438.   The House of Herman

A439.   As a singer at Club Dead

The Munsters Today continued

Q440. Grandpa was still a mad scientist and Igor still his pet bat. But there was now another resident in the dungeon, a skeleton he befriended in college. Name it.

Q441. Marilyn was a college student in the original series, but a high schooler here. While the 1964 Marilyn had no problem with dates (it was one look at Herman that scared them off), the 1988 Marilyn desperately wants a bigger bosom to attract boys. What size did she want to be?

Q442. Grave Diggers Mutual, "The Good Hands People," insured the Munster home at 1313 Mockingbird Lane and something else the family owned at 13-13th Avenue. What was it?

Murphy Brown
CBS, 1988–

Q443. A behind-the-scenes look at the preparations that go into making a TV newsmagazine (*F.Y.I.*) is the basis for this series. The Museum of Broadcast Arts and Sciences awarded *F.Y.I.* with what honor?

Q444. Murphy Brown is a hard-hitting investigative reporter who has a reputation for getting even with anyone who crosses her. But she does have a caring side ("I once fed the cat next door"), although people say she could never take care of a pet. Murphy, though, says she has. What kind of "pet" was it?

Q445. Aretha Franklin is Murphy's favorite singer; "Respect" is her favorite song, and she is fond of what particular type of flower?

Q446. Corky Sherwood is a reporter who can recite all the books of the Bible by heart. She was crowned Miss America at age nineteen, does stories like "Woody Woodpecker's 50th Birthday," and conducts interviews with "people" such as the San Diego chicken. In 1989 she won the Humboldt News Award for which one of her stories?

A440.   Leonard

A441.   36D

A442.   Munster Moor

Murphy Brown

A443.   Fifteen Years of Excellence in Journalism

A444.   "I got a Chia Pet to grow."

A445.   Sterling roses

A446.   "A Woman's Touch at West Point"

Murphy Brown continued

Q447. Frank Fontana joined *F.Y.I.* in 1977. He attended the Bishop Fallon High School for Boys and was a reporter for the *New York Times* before *F.Y.I.* Despite all his hard work, how does *TV Guide* have a tendency to list him?

Q448. Jim Dial is the respected if rather uptight senior anchor of *F.Y.I.* His TV career didn't begin with news but as the host of a local Channel 9 kid show. What was it called?

Q449. Elden Berneke, Murphy's personal house painter and nanny for her son, Avery, uses Murphy's good pantyhose to strain paint and buys his supplies at Ed's Paints. What is his favorite watering hole?

Q450. Phil's Bar, established in 1919, is the *F.Y.I.* gang's regular eatery. Murphy's favorite meal there is what?

My Living Doll
CBS, 1964–65

Q451. Dr. Carl Miller created AF 709, a beautiful female cyborg, for a project designed to send robots into outer space. Before it began, she was given to Bob McDonald, a psychologist, to mold her character, and he named her Rhoda while she posed as Carl's niece. Light provided Rhoda with power while her microsensors maintained her body temperature at 98.6 degrees. Where was her main power-off switch located?

Q452. Bob worked at the Cory Clinic where Rhoda posed as his secretary. Rhoda required no coffee breaks and could type how many words a minute?

My Mother the Car
NBC, 1965–66

Q453. Dave Crabtree was a lawyer whose dead mother had been reincarnated into the 1928 Porter he owned. What was his mother's first name?

A447. "Fred Fontana"

A448. *Poop Deck Pete and Cartoons Ahoy*

A449. The House Painter's Bar.

A450. A Phil Burger and Fries

My Living Doll

A451. On her right elbow

A452. 240

My Mother the Car

A453. Agatha

My Mother the Car continued

Q454. Dave paid $200 for the Porter, which still had its original brakes and carburetor. We could ask how many nuts, screws, and bolts did the carburetor have, but we won't. Instead, what brand of brakes did Mother have?

Q455. At night Dave covered Mother's radiator with a blanket so she wouldn't catch cold. He also bought her a used TV set (for $10) so she could watch her favorite TV show, which was what?

Q456. When Mother needed servicing, Dave would bring her to only one garage. Which one was it?

Newhart
CBS, 1982–90

Q457. Dick Loudon and his wife, Joanna, owned the Stratford Inn in Vermont. Joanna also sold real estate and Dick was a "How To" book author. After writing several such books, he decided to do one based on the inn. What did he call it?

Q458. Joanna and Bob also had TV shows on Channel 8. Bob hosted the daily program, *Vermont Today* and Joanna had a weekly real estate show that was originally called *Your House Is My House*. To improve ratings, what was it changed to?

Q459. George Utley, Dick's handyman, was a member of the Beaver Lodge and enjoyed bird watching at Johnny Kaye Lake. He also invented a board game. What did he call it?

Q460. A beautiful but quite spoiled and rather snooty heiress named Stephanie Vanderkellen took work as Dick's maid at the inn. She too had a series on Channel 8. What was it called?

Q461. Stephanie's boyfriend, Michael Harris, was the producer of her show. Insecure, he constantly showered her with gifts, but because there were not enough special holidays to give Stephanie presents, he created one (which comes between Valentine's Day and Easter). What day was it?

A454. Stops on a Dime Brakes. By the way, the carburetor had sixteen nuts, fourteen screws, and three bolts.

A455. *Jalopy Derby*

A456. Doc Benson's Auto Clinic

Newhart

A457. *Murder at the Stratley*

A458. *Hot Houses*

A459. Handyman: The Feel Good Game

A460. *Seein' Double*

A461. Cupcake Day

Newhart continued

Q462. The flounder was the town fish; the flying squirrel was the town bird. While the key to the city wouldn't open anything, it did do something. What?

Night Court
NBC, 1984–92

Q463. Harry Stone was a night-court arraignment judge in Manhattan. He was voted the Most Fascinating Judge in New York and was famous for his sentences. What were they?

Q464. Harry loved magic, was a Mel Torme fan, and had a specific coin as his lucky charm. What coin was it?

Q465. Christine Sullivan was the pretty legal aid attorney who said, "the most artistic people I get as clients are hookers with makeup skills." Easily exasperated, she often wondered why she became a lawyer. She had a car with Happy Face hubcaps and was a member of what support group?

Q466. Ian McKee was a New York street artist who found inspiration after meeting Christine. To show his gratitude, he painted a very large mural of her on a warehouse door. What did he call his masterpiece?

Q467. Ladies' man Dan Fielding earned his pay as a prosecuting attorney. He called his car "The Dan Mobile" and picked up girls at the Sticky Wickey. He also had a TV talk show. What was it called?

Q468. Dan Fielding was an assumed name. He was born on a rural farm in Louisiana and his parents named their kids and pigs after characters in books. What was Dan's real name?

Q469. Bull Shannon was the bald bailiff. He weighed 250 pounds and earned $320 a week. He got the nickname from his mother (she said "Bull" when she found out she was pregnant). What was Bull's real first name?

A462.   Start Willie Frye's tractor

Night Court

A463. $55 and time served

A464.   A Mercury-head dime

A465.   Ha Ha (Happy Alone, Happy Adults)

A466.   The Naked Body of Justice

A467.   *In Your Face*

A468.   Rheinhold Fielding Elmore

A469.   Nostradamus

Night Court continued

Q470. Bull lived next to a subway line in an apartment that had a concrete sofa ("durable, practical, and easy to patch") and a pet python. What was Bull's snake's name?

Q471. Roz Russell, the sassy bailiff, believed that her goal in life was to kick butt. But she didn't come by that belief in Harry's court; she learned it when she was a stewardess and encountered a group of annoying passengers. For what airline did Roz work?

Q472. Lisette was the pretty court stenographer who enjoyed knitting sweaters for birds, and also got a kick out of folding socks. She had a favorite lamp she called Sparky, a goldfish, and a plush giraffe. She called the giraffe Too Tall, but what did she call the goldfish?

The Odd Couple
ABC, 1970–74

Q473. Felix Unger was a neatnik; Oscar Madison a slob. They were divorced friends and roommates sharing an apartment in New York City. Nino's Italian Restaurant was their favorite eatery and they also managed to curtail their bickering long enough to write a song for singer Jaye P. Morgan. What did they call it?

Q474. Felix was born in Chicago, moved to Oklahoma, and grew up on a farm in upstate New York. He was a member of the Radio Actors Guild and in college had his own radio called *Felix*. On what real radio show did Felix appear as a kid?

Q475. During World War II, Felix was stationed in England and appeared in the army training film *How to Take a Shower* and originated the line "Men, don't let this happen to you." To what unit was he attached?

Q476. Felix also won the Silver Canteen Award during his service days for a song he wrote about Adolph Hitler. What was it called?

A470.   Bertha; later Harvey

A471.   Paramus Air Lines

A472.   Orca

The Odd Couple

A473.   "Happy and Peppy and Bursting With Love"

A474.   *Let's Pretend*

A475.   The 22nd Training Film Platoon, Educational Division of the Special Services

A476.   "To a Sour Kraut"

The Odd Couple continued

Q477. Gambling was Oscar's vice and Boston cream pie was his favorite dessert. While he did tend to put ketchup on everything, he also had a favorite dinner. What was it?

Q478. Oscar was born in Philadelphia at Our Lady of Angels Hospital. He attended the Langley Tippy-Toe Tap Dancing School as a kid and was enrolled in what high school?

One Day at a Time
CBS, 1975–84

Q479. The liberated Ann Romano and daughters Julie and Barbara resided at 1344 Hartford Drive in Indianapolis. Before owning her own ad agency, Ann worked for someone else. What was that company's name?

Q480. When Ann started her own agency, her first account was Startime Ice Cream. What was her biggest account at her previous job?

Q481. Julie, Ann's older and more troublesome daughter, had two favorite snacks. One was celery and ice cream. What was the other one?

Q482. Julie was rebellious, ran away from home, and wanted a career as a fashion designer. She never achieved her goal, but did find happiness when she married Max Horvath, a flight attendant who later tried his luck at writing. For what airline did Max work?

Q483. Younger sister Barbara attended Jefferson High School but dropped out of City College. She first worked for Quickie Burger, then at Olympic Sporting Goods, and finally at what travel agency?

Q484. The building super was Dwayne F. Schneider, a ladies' man who picked up girls at the Purple Pig Club. Dwayne's C.B. handle was "Super Stud" and he was a member of what lodge?

A477. Lasagna and French fries

A478. James K. Polk High

One Day at a Time

A479. Connors and Davenport

A480. Rutledge Toys

A481. Pickles and bananas

A482. PMA Airlines

A483. The Gonigan Travel Agency

A484. The Secret Order of the Beavers

Our Miss Brooks
CBS, 1952–56

Q485. Connie Brooks, a schoolteacher at Madison High School, was in love with shy Philip Boynton, who taught biology. She wished he would take "brave shots" and hoped to one day make a man out of him. Teaching English sometimes tired Connie out and she had invented a means of relaxing after a hard day that she called "School Teachers' B&B." Exactly what was this?

Q486. Philip carried jelly beans with him at all times. "The dextrose contained in them is one of the best sources of quick energy known to science." What color jelly beans was Connie most fond of?

Out of This World
Syndicated, 1987–91

Q487. Thirteen-year-old Evie Garland's mother was an earthling and her father, Troy, an alien from the planet Anterias. It was 1972 when Troy entered Natural Norman's Organic Ice Cream Parlor and saw Donna, a waitress. It was a love at first sight and they married shortly thereafter. What dessert did Troy order?

Q488. Evie attended Marlowe High School and her hangout was a soda shop called the Goodie Goodie. She played third string on the school's basketball team and had a plush cat. What did she call it?

Q489. Although Troy had not seen Evie since she was an infant (when he returned to his planet) he kept in touch with her through a genetic cube. By what term of endearment did Troy call Evie?

Q490. Evie's favorite breakfast was orange juice, hot cakes, and bacon, and her favorite movie star was Kevin Costner. She also loved to wear earrings and had what favorite TV soap opera?

Q491. Before becoming the mayor of Marlowe, California, Donna Garland first ran the Marlowe School for Gifted Children; then a catering service. What was the name of the company?

Our Miss Brooks

A485.   A bed and bath

A486.   The purple ones

Out of This World

A487.   A Raspberry Radish Rocket Ship

A488.   Twinky

A489.   "Earth Angel"

A490.   *All My Yesterday's Tomorrows*

A491.   Donna Delights Planning and Catering

Out of This World continued

Q492. Donna replaced Kyle X. Applegate as mayor when he lost the election by one vote. Kyle was a famous movie and TV star before entering politics, and on television he had three series. *Cowboy Kyle* was one of them; name one of the other two.

Q493. When Kyle was a movie star he portrayed Cowboy Kyle in such films as *The Good, the Bad and the Unattractive* and *Gunfight at the Pretty Good Corral*, which eventually turned into a TV series. Cowboy Kyle wore fancy shirts with ruffles and was assisted by Sheldon Moskowitz, the frontier dentist. Because of his role, Kyle had what off-the-set nickname?

The Patty Duke Show
ABC, 1963–66

Q494. Patty and Cathy Lane were identical cousins living in Brooklyn Heights. Patty was the typical American teenager and Cathy her sophisticated European counterpart. Star Patty Duke also played a third cousin, a blond bombshell version of the two girls who hailed from Atlanta. Patty called her a "Confederate Cleopatra," but what was her real name?

Q495. The Lane family, which also included father Martin, mother Natalie, and brother Ross, lived at 8 Remsen Drive in a house that dated back to the days of George Washington. Who built the place in 1720?

Q496. When Patty thought she could become a teenage sensation as a writer, she wrote a book combining "love, war, poverty, death, and cooking recipes." What did she title it?

Q497. Patty Duke was given the opportunity to sing in several episodes. In one, she acquired a job at the Pink Percolator, a coffeehouse that serves seventy-five different kinds of coffee. Under what name did she work?

A492. *The Floridian* or *Mosquito Man*

A493. "The Ruffleman"

The Patty Duke Show

A494. Betsy Lane

A495. Adam Prescott, whose son, Jonathan, served under Gen. George Washington

A496. *I Was a Teenage Teenager.*

A497. Pittsburgh Patty

The Patty Duke Show *continued*

Q498. Before coming to America, Cathy lived in Scotland where she attended a private school, where she was the debating champion. What was the name of the school?

Q499. Patty's father, Martin, was the managing editor of the New York *Chronicle* while Cathy's father, Martin's twin, was its foreign correspondent. What paper was in direct competition with the *Chronicle*?

The People's Choice
NBC, 1955–58

Q500. Sock Miller, a councilman in the Fifth District of New City, California, lived in a trailer camp with his Aunt Gus and basset hound Cleo. Before entering politics, Sock was an ornithologist for the Bureau of Fish and Wildlife whose job was to "follow the birds" and file reports on their migratory habits. How many miles had Sock logged following birds?

Q501. When we first met Sock he was tracking down the Yellow-Necked Nuthatch. What was his last assignment before becoming a councilman?

Q502. Sock married Mandy Peoples, the mayor's daughter, in later episodes. What did Mayor Peoples call Sock?

Perfect Strangers
ABC, 1986–93

Q503. Balki Bartokomous hailed from a Mediterranean island called Mypos. Sheepherding was the number one occupation there and the national debt was $635. What animal graced Myposian money?

Q504. When Balki discovered that he had an American cousin (Larry Appleton) living in Chicago, he set out to find him and eventually became his roommate. While Cousin Larry was not of full Myposian blood, how Myposian was he?

A498.   Mrs. Tutles of Mountain Briar

A499.   The *Record*

The People's Choice

A500.   80,000

A501.   To find out why the Rose-breasted Grosbeak was laying smaller eggs this season.

A502.   "Nature Boy"

Perfect Strangers

A503.   A cow

A504.   One sixty-fourth

Perfect Strangers continued

Q505. Balki relished yak links for breakfast and his favorite meal was eel wrapped in grape leaves and sheepherder's bread with a side dish of Ding Ding Mac-Mood (pig snout). He was also a gourmet cook and the best bibibobaca baker on Mypos. What type of dessert was bibibobaca?

Q506. On Mypos, Balki had several pets: a sheep (Dimitri), a three-hundred-pound turtle (Bibby), a horse (Trodsky), and a dog. What did he call the dog?

Q507. Larry was born in May and as a kid had a dog named Spot. His catchphrase was "Oh, My Lord" and he gargled to the tune of what specific song?

Q508. In last-season episodes, Larry married Jennifer and Balki wed her roommate, Mary Anne. The two cousins also become parents. Larry and Jennifer named their son Tucker; what did Balki and Mary Anne name theirs?

The Phil Silvers Show (Sgt. Bilko)
CBS, 1955–59

Q509. The series was originally called *You'll Never Get Rich* and dealt with the moneymaking schemes of endlessly crafty Ernest Bilko, a sergeant with the Company B Motor Pool at Fort Baxter, Kansas. His "career," however, began during World War II, when he was stationed in New Guinea. What was his first scam?

Q510. Bilko moved on to the 24th Division motor pool. What division was he with on New Guinea?

Q511. The base cook, Rupert Ritzik, was Bilko's main patsy. Ritzik read comic books, believed in flying saucers, and was a big fan of TV space shows. What was his favorite series?

A505. Cream puff

A506. Koos Koos

A507. "Moon River"

A508. Robespierre Boinkie

The Phil Silvers Show

A509. Selling USO girls nylons at $5 a pair

A510. The 38th

A511. *Captain Dan, Space Man*

The Powers That Be
NBC, 1992–93

Q512. The Powers were a dysfunctional political family. Bill was a senator; ambitious Margaret, his wife, was yearning to become a First Lady; and their daughter, Caitlin, was married to Theodore, a wimpy congressman. Bill enjoyed Jerry Lewis movies, blueberry muffins, and a martini each night. He had a dog named Little Dickens and loved what one particular song?

Q513. Caitlin had a fear of brunch, allowed only Mr. Sidney to cut her hair, and loved to wear pink. What did she do before each political party? .

Q514. Caitlin, who called her mother "Mummy," was pretty, self-serving, and vain. But she also did charity work. What was her favorite charity?

Roc
Fox, 1991–

Q515. Roc Emerson is a hardworking garbage man with a dream—to own a semidetached house. But until that time comes he lives in an attached house with his wife, Eleanor; his father, Andrew; and his brother, Joey. Roc reads yesterday's news today and has a home furnished mostly with "perks" (items other people discarded that Roc found on his route). It is a hard job, though. How many garbage cans does Roc have to empty to make $2,000?

Q516. Roc's favorite watering hole is Charlene's Bar, but he has coffee with his coworkers at the shop next to the depot. What are either the first or second season names for the coffee shop?

The Powers That Be

A512. "Supercalifragalisticexpialidocious"

A513. Buy a dress one size too small and starve herself until she fit into it.

A514. The Halfway House for Congressmen's Wives

Roc

A515. 175,214

A516. The Dump (first season), then the Landfill

Roseanne
ABC, 1988–

Q517. Roseanne Harris and Dan Conner met in Lanford High School. They dated, married shortly after graduation, set up housekeeping at 714 Delaware Street, and became the parents of three children (Becky, Darlene, and D.J.). Dan's prized possession is his Harley-Davidson motorcycle and he owned a construction company. What did he call it?

Q518. Roseanne held a number of jobs: assembly-line worker, telephone solicitor, order taker, clean-up lady, waitress, and diner owner. She worked the assembly line at Wellman Plastics and was a waitress at Rodbell's Luncheonette. What product did she sell over the phone?

Q519. Sweet and feminine Becky is the oldest child. Her favorite color is red and she enjoys Dannon yogurt. To earn extra money Becky became a cashier at what supermarket?

Q520. Sister Darlene is a tomboy and nasty. She seems to live in her own world and is closer to her father than to her mother. She loves sports and what particular brand of breakfast cereal?

Q521. D.J., the youngest child, has a collection of doll heads and a talent for doing something. Roseanne doesn't know how he manages to do it, but she uses oil to remedy the situation. What "talent" does D.J. have?

Seinfeld
NBC, 1990–

Q522. Events in the daily life of stand-up comedian Jerry Seinfeld can best describe this series. Jerry and his friends Elaine, George, and neighbor across the hall Kramer eat frequently at "The Restaurant," as it is noted in establishing scenes. There is no lettering on the windows in these scenes either. However, an inside shot looking out indicates "The Restaurant" is really what eatery?

Roseanne

A517.   4 Aces Construction

A518.   *Discount House* magazine

A519.   The Buy 'n' Bag

A520.   Fruit Rings

A521.   Getting his head stuck in drawers. "He's got a talent for it," says Roseanne.

Seinfeld

A522.   Monk's Cafe

Seinfeld continued

Q523. Elaine has the nickname "Nip" around her office after she decided to give a Christmas card of herself to her friends. She didn't realize that her blouse was open at the time and her nipple was showing; neither did the photographer who took the picture. Who snapped the famous "Nip" picture of Elaine?

Q524. When Kramer got the show business bug and thought he could become a great actor, he moved to Hollywood. Although his dream was never realized, Kramer did manage to land a role on *Murphy Brown*. What part did he play?

Silver Spoons
NBC/Syndicated, 1982–88

Q525. Thirty-two-year-old Edward Stratton III was a divorced millionaire who ran the Eddie Toys division of Stratton Industries, a company founded by his great-grandfather, "a banana head who became rich by accident." How did this "banana head" become rich?

Q526. Eddie Toys had its successes and its failures. One of the biggest disasters was a board game that sold six of the fifty thousand units that were produced—and two were returned. What was the game called?

Q527. Now married to Kate, Edward was the father of a twelve-year-old boy named Ricky from his first marriage to Evelyn. Kate was a shoe nut who worried about matching everything with her shoes. When Kate became an active part of Eddie Toys she marketed a Viking doll with an attitude problem. What did she call the doll?

The Simpsons
Fox, 1990–

Q528. The Simpsons are a not-so-typical American cartoon family who live in the small town of Springfield. Homer, the father, is an overweight safety inspector at the local power plant. In what section does he work?

A523.　Kramer

A524.　"Steve Snell," one of Murphy's parade of secretaries

Silver Spoons

A525.　He came up with a rubber inner tube, one year before the invention of the car, as a means of staying afloat in the water when he went to the beach. When Ford made his first car, he used the tube.

A526.　Endangered Species

A527.　The Viking Warrior

The Simpsons

A528.　Sector 76

The Simpsons *continued*

Q529. Homer is married to Marge, a thirty-four-year-old blue-beehived housewife and the mother of Bart, Lisa, and Maggie. Bart, TV's bad boy, is the undefeated champ of the video game Slug Fest and his favorite television show is *Krusty the Clown*. He has two pets, a frog and a dog. The dog is called Santa's Little Helper; what did Bart name the frog?

Q530. Practical joke–playing Bart spends much time in the principal's office. He is also a member of the Krusty the Clown fan club and allergic to what specific food?

Q531. Precocious middle child Lisa is a budding saxophone player, reads *Teen Screen* and *Teen Steam* magazines and, while she too watches Krusty the Clown, her favorite TV show is a very violent cartoon. What is it?

Small Wonder
Syndicated, 1985–89

Q532. Short for Voice Input Child Identicate, Vicki was a robot who was created by Ted Lawson as part of a secret experiment to help handicapped children. Ted lived with his wife Joanie and son Jamie in Los Angeles and passed off Vicki (made of plastic, wires, transistors, and micro chips) as his adopted daughter. What invention of Ted's gave Vicki life?

Q533. Vicki had a built-in micro generator and possessed incredible strength. Her brown eyes were solar cells that provide power. What command turned Vicki off?

Q534. Joanie so loved Vicki that she often forgot that the robot was not human. Joanie had dinner ready each night at 6:30 and called leftovers "reruns." "That's nice" was her catchphrase and as a kid she had a pet canary. What did she call it?

A529. Froggie

A530. Butterscotch

A531. *The Itchy and Scratchy Show*

Small Wonder

A532. The Waffer Scale Integration System

A533. Stop

A534. Tweet Tweet

Step by Step
ABC, 1991–

Q535. Carol, a widowed hairdresser with three kids (Dana, Karen and Mark), and Frank, a divorced construction company owner with three kids (Alicia, J.T. and Brendon), marry and attempt to build a new life step by step. They met when Frank came to Carol for a haircut and were married in Jamaica three months later. Where in Jamaica was the ceremony?

Q536. "I'm what the guys call a babe," says fourteen-year-old Karen, often mistaken for a model ("But I'm not"). She is always fashionably dressed and really wants to become a model. Carol believes that her daughter's obsession with herself is her (Carol's) fault because she gave Karen what?

Q537. Fifteen-year-old Dana is Carol's oldest, a straight A student and sensitive to the fact that she has a small bustline. Dana writes for her school newspaper and is the assistant manager of what after-school hangout?

Q538. "You Little Criminal" is one of Dana's "terms of endearment" for Alicia, Frank's pretty twelve-year-old daughter. Alicia is a tomboy, has great potential for the construction business, and had been a member of what all-girl band?

Q539. In 1971 Carol was a contestant in the Miss Small Curd Cottage Cheese Beauty Pageant. She was crowned First Runner-Up. To whom did she lose the title?

Q540. Frank uses a construction site story to explain aspects of the world to the kids. He was president of the Tile and Grout Association and is also a member of what lodge?

Taxi
ABC/NBC, 1978–83

Q541. Louie DePalma was the nasty, snide dispatcher for the Sunshine Cab Company in Manhattan. His office was called the Cage and he believed all his drivers to be losers. According to Louie, only one cabbie made it out and so far had not returned. Who was it?

Step by Step

A535.   The Wedding Shack

A536.   A Brooke Shields doll

A537.   The '50s Cafe

A538.   Chicks with Attitudes

A539.   "I lost to a girl with bigger curds."

A540.   The Mallard Lodge

Taxi

A541.   James Caan—"But he'll be back. They all come back."

Taxi *continued*

Q542. Louie lived for his job at the company and had been there fifteen years, first as a driver, then as the dispatcher. He liked bookings high and would appreciate a call if a cabbie cannot make his shift. But he hated what one word, a word he didn't want to hear ("Never, never say the word!")?

Q543. Lecherous, money-worshipping Louie considered himself a ladies' man even though cabbie Alex Reiger remarked, "If God had a reason for creating snakes, lice, and vermin, He had a reason for creating Louie." Lady cabbie Elaine Nardo was often the unencouraged object of Louie's lust. What did he call her breasts?

Q544. Cabbie Bobby Wheeler, an aspiring actor who starred in a one-man play called *Charles Darwin Tonight*, also played the role of Skip on what TV soap opera?

Q545. James Caldwell, a once brilliant Harvard student who became somewhat spaced-out on drugs and believed he is living in the 1960s, changed his name to Jim Ignatowski when he believed "Star Child" was Ignatowski spelled backward. In 1968 he was ordained as Reverend Jim. In what Church was he a minister?

That Girl
ABC, 1966–71

Q546. "That Girl" was Ann Marie, a small-towner who came to the big city to further her career as an actress. Earlier she had won a medal as Best Actress at Camp Winnepoo and was a member of her college drama club. While not having the greatest qualifications, she was still accepted into what drama school?

Q547. Acting jobs were not always easy to come by and Ann took any one she could find to help pay the bills. She worked as a model, door-to-door shoe salesgirl, and a spokesgirl for a fast food chicken product. What was she?

Q548. Ann's TV debut was on an unnamed show playing a bank teller. Her most embarrassing moment also happened on television. What was it?

A542.   Accident

A543.   Headlights

A544.   *For Better, For Worse*

A545.   The Church of the Peaceful

That Girl

A546.   The Benedict Workshop of the Dramatic Arts

A547.   "Miss Chicken Big" for Chicken Big, Inc.

A548.   She played a corpse and opened her eyes on camera on live TV.

That Girl continued

Q549. Lou Marie, Ann's father, disapproved of her career until he let her direct his local stage group at the Brewster Country Club. Lou had become famous in Brewster for his rendition of what vaudeville song?

Three's Company
ABC, 1977–84

Q550. Janet Wood, Chrissy Snow, and Jack Tripper shared Apartment 201 at the Ropers' Apartment House in California. Janet was a store manager, Chrissy worked as a secretary, and Jack was a cooking student who pretended to be gay to live in the apartment and was studying French cuisine. ("You're looking at the Galloping Gourmet of 1980"). What cooking school was he attending?

Q551. Janet was born in Massachusetts and had a tendency to nag a lot. She was first a salesgirl, then the manager of what store?

Q552. Sexy Chrissy Snow was born on December 25. She was very sweet and trusting and her real name was Christmas Snow. To supplement her income as a secretary, she took a second job selling cosmetics. What was the name of the products?

The Tony Randall Show
ABC/CBS, 1976–78

Q553. Walter Oliver Franklin was a widower and the father of two children, Roberta and Oliver, Jr. Walter was born on June 17 and lived in Philadelphia. He was a less-than-magisterial judge with what court system?

Q554. To earn extra money, Walter took a job teaching law at a less-than-prestigious school. Name it.

A549.   "Minnie the Moocher"

Three's Company

A550.   The L.A. Technical School

A551.   The Arcade Florist Shop

A552.   Easy Time Cosmetics

The Tony Randall Show

A553.   The Court of Common Pleas

A554.   Ed's School of Law

Too Close for Comfort
ABC/Syndicated, 1980–86

Q555. Henry Rush, wife, Muriel, and grown daughters, Jackie and Sarah, lived in a red Victorian house in San Francisco. Henry was a cartoonist and creator of the comic book "Cosmic Cow," a space crime fighter. What was his biggest challenge when sketching Cosmic Cow?

Q556. In order to keep tabs on Jackie and Sarah, Henry rented them the downstairs apartment for how much a month?

Q557. Sarah, a college student, took various part-time jobs to pay her half of the rent. She got her first job as a "wench waitress" because she had a figure that fit the available costume. What was the bar called?

Q558. Henry's daily aggravation stemmed not only from keeping tabs on Jackie and Sarah, but also from his tenant, Monroe Ficus, a lost soul who sort of attached himself to Sarah. Monroe worked as a security guard and was once named Officer April for catching a shoplifter. Where did Monroe work?

227
NBC, 1985–90

Q559. Housewife Mary Jenkins was president of the tenant's association of an apartment house at 227 in Washington. Her husband, Lester, was an engineer with the Stumer and Nathan Construction Company. Where did Mary work?

Q560. To supplement her weekly allowance, daughter Brenda became a burger bagger at what fast food store?

Q561. Of all the residents at 227, the most colorful was beautiful Sandra Clark, who knew she was a threat to other men's wives and used her wiles to get men to do what she wanted. Sandra had a favorite letter of the alphabet. What is it?

Q562. Sandra came to 227 as a college student. She was a bombshell then and had a nickname. What was it?

Too Close for Comfort

A555.   "To draw an udder so it is not offensive."

A556. $300

A557.   The Fox and Hound

A558.   Riverwood Shopping Mall

227

A559.   Winslow Travel Agency

A560.   Billy Bob's Burger Barge

A561.   "M—for money, men, and me."

A562.   "Sparkles"

Webster
ABC/Syndicated, 1983–88

Q563. Seven-year-old Webster Long resided with his godfather, George Papadopolis, and George's wife, Katherine. Webster kept his "menstoes" (mementos) in an old cigar box and he had a teddy bear, two frogs, a snake, and a home-made robot. He called the teddy bear Teddy, but what was his name for the robot?

Q564. Webster ate Sugar Sweeties cereal for breakfast, played trumpet in the school band, and enjoyed feeding the pigeons in the park. He had named a number of them but had a favorite. Which one was it?

Welcome Back, Kotter
ABC, 1975–79

Q565. Gabe Kotter was a graduate of James Buchanan High School who returned ten years later to teach Special Guidance Remedial Academics to a class of delinquents known as Sweathogs (Vinnie Barbarino, Juan Epstein, Freddy Washington, and Arnold Horshack). Before becoming a teacher, Gabe had aspired to become a comedian. Where did he perform his stand-up routines?

Q566. There were three Mary Johnsons at Buchanan High. The plain and sensitive Mary Johnson was Arnold's girlfriend. What were the other two Mary Johnsons called?

Q567. While the Sweathogs were hardly students, they were street smart and knew how to handle themselves on the sidewalks of Brooklyn. When they pooled their resources to buy a car, what did they call it?

Webster

A563.   Mr. Spielberg

A564.   Charlie

Welcome Back, Kotter

A565.   The Comedy Connection Club

A566.   Mary the cheerleader; Mary the athlete

A567.   The Sweatmobile

What's Happening!!

ABC, 1976–79

Q568. Raj, Dwayne, and Rerun were three friends who lived in Southern California and attended Jefferson High School. Raj had ambitions to become a writer and was editor of the school newspaper, the *Gazette*. "Mr. Beaver Builds a Dam and Saves the Town of Gum Drop Falls" was the title of the first story Raj wrote. What magazine published it?

Q569. Rerun's real name was Freddie Stubbs. His nickname came from his habit of repeating in summer school what he should have learned in the fall. Before becoming a page at KABC-TV, Rerun was a member of what rock group?

Who's the Boss?

ABC, 1984–92

Q570. Tony Micelli, a widower and the father of a young girl, Samantha, worked as the housekeeper to Angela Bower, a high-powered ad exec and divorcée with a young son, Jonathan. Before a career-ending injury, Tony was a professional ball player and was second baseman for two seasons. For what team did Tony play?

Q571. Samantha was affectionately called Sam. French toast was her favorite breakfast and she called it "Mr. Frenchie." Pasta, which she referred to as "Mr. Linguini," was her favorite dinner. She also had a favorite plush teddy bear. What was her name for it?

Q572. Before beginning her own ad company, the Angela Bower Agency, Angela was the president of another agency in Manhattan. Name the one she headed.

Q573. As a teenager, Angela attended the Montague Academy for Girls. While not as popular as she would have liked to be (she called herself a geek because she was not as busty as the other girls), she did manage to find some happiness as a member of what singing group?

What's Happening!!

A568.   *Little Miss Muffet*

A569.   The Rockets

Who's the Boss?

A570.   St. Louis Cardinals

A571.   Freddy Fuzzy Face

A572.   Wallace and McQuade

A573.   The Curlets

Who's the Boss? continued

Q574. Mona, Angela's ultrasexy mother and her assistant at the ad agency, was rather well developed and constantly reminded her daughter that she lacks cleavage. What was the "term of endearment" Mona's mother had for her?

WKRP in Cincinnati
CBS, 1978–82

Q575. WKRP was a 5,000 watt AM radio station located on the ninth floor of the Flem Building. The highest rating it ever achieved was number 14 and the "Big Guy," Arthur Carlson, ran the station for his overbearing mother. Blond bombshell Jennifer Marlowe, the highest paid employee at the station, worked as the receptionist. How much a year did she make?

Q576. Jennifer, described by other women as "the best-looking woman I have ever seen," would only date older men (she feels safer with them) and lived in a gorgeous apartment with a unique doorbell. When rung, what song did it play?

Q577. The station couldn't afford a news van so Les Nessman, the station's lovably nerdy news director, used his motor scooter as the WKRP mobile news unit. Les was very proud of his news broadcasts, especially the hog reports segment. What award had Les won for these reports?

Q578. Venus Flytrap was the late night disc jockey. His real name was Gordon Sims, but he was in hiding and changed his named after going AWOL. How long was Gordon in the army before he deserted?

Q579. *WKRP's* 1978 Thanksgiving episode was perhaps the most famous one of any series, in which Arthur devised a plan to wish his listeners a happy holiday and hired a helicopter with a banner that read "Happy Thanksgiving." Passing over a mall, he dropped live turkeys from two thousand feet. Shoppers begin running for their lives as the turkeys hit the ground like wet bags of cement. "As God is my witness," Arthur said, "I thought turkeys could fly." What was the name of the mall that was bombarded with turkeys?

A574. "All boobs and no brains."

WKRP in Cincinnati

A575. $24,000

A576. "Fly Me to the Moon"

A577. The Silver Sow Award

A578. Ten months and 29 days

A579. The Pine Dale Shopping Mall

CHAPTER

2

Drama and Adventure

The A-Team
NBC, 1983–87

Q580. Hannibal Smith, B.A. Baracus, H.M. Murdock, and Templeton Peck were the A-Team, Vietnam buddies wanted by the army, who helped people in trouble. What military leader framed the A-Team for robbing the bank of Hanoi?

Q581. B.A. stood for Bad Attitude and he lived up to that name although he was a pussycat around children. What was the nickname his mother gave him?

Q582. Murdock lived in the psychiatric ward of the VA Hospital in Los Angeles and was believed to be suffering from paranoid delusions. What key word triggered his aggression?

Q583. Although Murdock and B.A. appeared to have nothing in common and B.A. honestly believed Murdock to be crazy, they did share one thing—the same blood type. What type was it?

Q584. Murdock had two heroes, one from an old TV show, the other the spokesman for a hamburger food chain. Name either one of them.

Q585. Templeton, nicknamed "Face," was raised in an orphanage and learned most of his cons by watching TV. He used that knowledge to scrounge for the team what they needed. What TV series was so helpful to Face?

The A-Team

A580.   Col. Samuel Morrison

A581.   "Scooter"

A582.   Ammonia

A583.   A-B Negative

A584.   *The Range Rider* or Captain Bellybuster of Burger Heaven

A585.   *Dragnet*

Adventures in Paradise
ABC, 1959–62

Q586. Adam Troy was a Korean War veteran who owned a schooner named the *Tiki* and earned a living by ferrying passengers and cargo in Tahiti. The schooner had a temperamental engine. What did Troy call the engine?

Q587. While Adam did set sail for exotic adventures, he had a home base on Tahiti. Where did he anchor the *Tiki* and what was his address?

Q588. In last-season episodes, Clay Baker jumped ship to become the owner of a hotel. He also made a reputation for himself as a bartender. Name the two drinks for which he was famous.

Airwolf
CBS, 1984–86

Q589. Airwolf was an awesome attack helicopter piloted by Stringfellow Hawke. To protect the chopper from the government officials who wanted it back, Hawke had hidden it in a secluded area in California. What did he call Airwolf's hiding place?

Q590. Hawke liked privacy and lived in a remote section of California with a dog. Name his companion.

Q591. Airwolf was built by the U.S. Government, then stolen and held hostage by Hawke until his brother, listed as missing in Vietnam, was located. What was Airwolf's file number?

Q592. Airwolf was a Bell 222 helicopter and equipped with computers, missiles, and chain guns in its wings. What was its cruising speed?

Q593. Hawke's partner, Dominic Santini, ran his own air charter service from the Municipal Airport in California. On what island was Dom born?

Adventures in Paradise

A586. "The Lady"

A587. The *Tiki* is anchored at the Papeete Harbor; Troy's address is the Schooner *Tiki*.

A588. Tahitian Madness and the Polynesian Rainmaker

Airwolf

A589. Valley of the Gods

A590. Tet

A591. A56-7W

A592. 300 knots

A593. San Remo

The Avengers
ABC, 1966–69

Q594. Debonair British agent John Steed exuded Old World charm, drove a vintage Bentley, and took his coffee with three sugars. He also had an Achilles' heel. What was it?

Q595. The sexy, totally emancipated Emma Peel partnered with Steed for the sheer love of adventure. Emma never worked; she inherited what company from her late father?

Q596. "Better Bridge Through Applied Mathematics" was the famous article Emma wrote for the June issue of what magazine?

Q597. Before Steed was teamed with the shapely Tara King, Emma Peel's replacement, he "met" her when she accidentally tackled him during a training exercise assignment. What was Tara's agent recruiting number?

Banacek
NBC, 1972–74

Q598. Thomas Banacek, a free-lance, Boston-based insurance investigator who recovered lost or stolen objects, also operated his own business. What was it?

Q599. For his research, Banacek used the Recovery and Rewards section of what paper?

Q600. Carlie Kirkland, Banacek's competitor, worked in what department of the Boston Insurance Company?

Batman
ABC, 1966–68

Q601. Millionaire Bruce Wayne and his youthful ward, Dick Grayson, lived at stately Wayne Manor with Alfred, their ever-faithful butler. Batman and Robin never mixed crimefighting with eating; however, after each assignment, they were treated to what meal by Alfred?

The Avengers

A594.   The opposite sex

A595.   Knight Industries

A596.   *The Bridge Players International Guide*

A597.   Agent 69

Banacek

A598.   T. Banacek—Restorations

A599.   *The Assurance Reports*

A600.   Property and Recovery Division

Batman

A601.   Milk and sandwiches

Batman continued

Q602. While Batman did have a fun side (for example, he invented a dance called the Batusi), he could not abide one thing. What was it?

Q603. Assisting Batman and Robin was Barbara Gordon, alias Batgirl. While Barbara worked for the Gotham City library, she was also chairperson of what Gotham City committee?

Q604. Alfred was the only one to know the true identities of Batman and Robin. He also assisted them in the field. When the phone rang at Wayne Manor, what were the words Alfred used to answer it?

Q605. Barbara lived in midtown Gotham City in Apartment 8A with her pet bird. What was its name?

Q606. As Batgirl, Barbara received the first Gotham City Female Crime Fighting and Fashion Award. What was the award called?

Baywatch
NBC/Syndicated, 1989–

Q607. Mitch Buchannan originally shared outpost tower 27 with Jill Riley. While attempting to save swimmers from a shark sighting, Jill, a lifeguard with Baywatch, was attacked by the animals and suffered massive internal injuries. She never recovered and mentioned that she never had the opportunity to finish reading what book that she began as a teenager?

Q608. After breaking up with her husband, Mitch, Gayle left California for a job in another state. At what fast food place did she find employment?

Q609. Lifeguard Shauni McClain attended South Central High School and received $50 from her parents for every A on her report card. Shauni uses a specific brand of sun block when working on the beach. Name it.

A602. Being called a coward

A603. The Anti-Littering Committee

A604. "Stately Wayne Manor"

A605. Charlie

A606. The Battie

Baywatch

A607. *Wuthering Heights*

A608. Captain Cluck's Chicken and Fixin' Franchises

A609. "Bohemian Love"

Baywatch *continued*

Q610. Summer Quinn is a beautiful lifeguard trainee who replaced Shauni in 1992. What was Summer's greatest fear during training?

Beauty and the Beast
CBS, 1987–90

Q611. The subterranean world beneath the New York subway system was home to Vincent, the beast, and Father, the leader of a group of misfit people. In this world without telephones, TV's or radios, how did the people keep in contact with one another?

Q612. The tunnels where this underground society lived led to all areas of the city, giving them access to the outside world. Which part of this subterranean community was most dangerous for these people?

Q613. The people of the underworld had contacts in the world above who kept their secret and assisted them. What were these people called?

Q614. In the final episode, Vincent (the beast of the title), had a son by Catherine Chandler (beauty). What did Vincent name his son?

Beverly Hills, 90210
Fox, 1990–

Q615. Brenda and Brandon Walsh are sixteen-year-old fraternal twins who now attend West Beverly Hills High. Brenda is the older twin; by how much?

Q616. Brenda's favorite TV show is *Keep It Together*, but it was Brandon who landed a role on it. When Brenda had to substitute for Brandon at the Peach Pit as a waitress, what name did she use?

Q617. When the family lived in Minnesota, Brenda and Brandon were both straight A students. Brenda was a member of the drama club and Brandon wrote for the school newspaper. What was Brandon called at school?

A610.   Diving off the 100-foot pier

Beauty and the Beast

A611.   Tapping on the underground pipes that run throughout the city

A612.   Prince Street on Manhattan's lower East Side

A613.   Helpers

A614.   Jacob

Beverly Hills, 90210

A615.   Four minutes

A616.   Laverne

A617.   Mr. Popularity

Beverly Hills, 90210 continued

Q618. As a kid Brenda had two plush toys—a horse and a lion. She called the lion "Mr. Lion." What did she call the horse?

Q619. Jim, Brenda and Brandon's father, calls Brandon "Big Guy." What does he call Brenda?

The Bionic Woman
ABC/NBC, 1976–78

Q620. "The Home of American Astronaut Steve Austin" was the sign one saw on entering this small town in California where Jaime Sommers, the Bionic Woman of the title, also lived. Name the town.

Q621. Days before her almost fatal skydiving accident, tennis pro Jaime Sommers was scheduled to play what opponent in Spain?

Q622. Rudy Wells, the bionic surgeon responsible for Jaime's upkeep, invented a taffy-like substance that could, in essence, give anybody bionic powers. The substance was deadly, however, if taken in large doses. What did Dr. Wells call his discovery?

Q623. In addition to the role of Jaime Sommers, Lindsay Wagner played a girl who, through plastic surgery, became a Jaime Sommers lookalike. This Jaime, however, was up to no good, and sought the secret of the real Jaime's powers. What was her name?

B.J. and the Bear
NBC, 1979–81

Q624. B.J. McKay was a trucker who traveled with his simian companion, Bear, across the country. B.J. would haul anything legal anywhere for how much a mile?

Q625. B.J. was a POW in Vietnam when he found Bear (Bear would bring him food to help him survive). After whom did B.J. name Bear?

A618. Mr. Pony

A619. "Beautiful"

The Bionic Woman

A620. Ojai

A621. Billie Jean King

A622. Hydrazene

A623. Lisa Galloway

B.J. and the Bear

A624. $1.50

A625. After Paul "Bear" Bryant, whom B.J. considered to be a great football coach

B.J. and the Bear continued

Q626. B.J. also had another name for Bear and he often called him by this. What was it?

Q627. B.J. played the sax and he once did so with a band. Name the band.

Q628. When B.J. set up his own business (Bear Enterprises) he did so over a bar where two of his truckers, twins Geri and Teri, worked. What was the name of the bar?

Q629. One of B.J.'s seven lady truckers (last-season episodes) had a crush on him, but exclaimed "B.J. sees me only as a girl who can drive a rig and fix a flat tire." Not as feminine as the other girls, she also had what B.J. calls "a smart mouth." Who was she?

Bourbon Street Beat
ABC, 1959–60

Q630. The detective firm of Randolph and Calhoun was located on Bourbon Street in the French Quarter of New Orleans. Name the famous nightclub located next to it.

Q631. Rex Randolph, the senior partner, was an Ivy League man and loved to cook. Before becoming Rex's partner, Cal Calhoun was a lieutenant with what police department?

Q632. The firm's receptionist, Melody Lee Mercer, yearned to become a detective. She was born in Louisiana and won a 1958 beauty pageant. What title was it?

Q633. Kenny Madison was a part-time detective who works for Rex. He was studying to become a lawyer and attended what university?

Buck Rogers in the 25th Century
NBC, 1979–81

Q634. After drifting in space for almost five hundred years, Buck's rocket, the Ranger III, was found by Princess Ardella, the commander of a two-mile-wide space craft. What was the name of her ship?

A626. "The Kid"

A627. Ghettoway City

A628. Phil's Disco

A629. Callie

Bourbon Street Beat

A630. The Old Absinthe House

A631. Pelican Point P.D.

A632. Miss U.S.A. in the 1958 Miss Universe Pageant

A633. Tulane

Buck Rogers in the 25th Century

A634. The King's Flagship Draconia

Buck Rogers in the 25th Century continued

Q635. Finding that he could not go back to his time, Buck joined Wilma Deering and Dr. Elias Huer to help with their future. What did Buck become a member of?

Q636. In this future world the retirement age had risen to eighty-five and America had a new capital. What was it?

Charlie's Angels
ABC, 1976–81

Q637. Sabrina Duncan, Jill Munroe, and Kelly Garrett were the original "Charlie's Angels." Each was a former officer with the L.A.P.D. Jill's sister, Kris Munroe, replaced her; Tiffany Welles replaced Sabrina; and Julie Rogers replaced Tiffany. Julie was also an L.A.P.D. officer, but what police departments did Tiffany and Kris represent?

Q638. The angels never saw their employer. Charlie contacted them via a telephone (usually heard over a speaker phone) or through his representative, John Bosley. What company did Charlies own that required the services of three angels?

China Beach
ABC, 1988–91

Q639. The U.S. Armed Forces R&R facility in Danang was the 510 Evac Hospital, 63rd Division. The unit was unable to handle critical neurological surgery, but took care of virtually everything else. How many beds and how many surgical units were there?

Q640. Colleen McMurphy was a triage nurse who volunteered for service in Vietnam. What was she called when she first arrived on China Beach?

Q641. Colleen desperately wanted to do her job while at the same time overcome her feelings of frustration. In all the time she spent on China Beach, she had only one wish. What was it?

A635. The Third Force of the Earth Directorate

A636. New Chicago

Charlie's Angels

A637. Tiffany (Boston), Kris (San Francisco)

A638. Townsend Investigations or the Townsend Detective Agency

China Beach

A639. 180 beds, 33 surgical units

A640. F.N.G. (Fairly New Guy)

A641. A day without choppers (which brought the wounded)

China Beach continued

Q642. K.C. was the only civilian on China Beach. She was a high-priced prostitute and charged how much an hour?

Q643. K.C. was from Kansas City, but the K.C. stood for something else—K.C.'s real name. What was it?

Q644. Colleen and Karen first saw each other in the women's shower. K.C. noticed Colleen staring at her navel and said what to her?

Q645. Something made K.C. feel safe as a child; she would snuggle under the bed covers and gain a sense of safety. On China Beach this same thing provided her with the only sense of safety she could feel amid the devastation that surrounded her. What was it?

Q646. Boonewell "Boonie" Lanier was with the First Marine Division, Icor, on China Beach. What did he always call K.C.?

Q647. Laurette Barber was a single-dancer with the USO touring Vietnam. Although it was not part of her job, she helped Colleen in times of emergency. Laurette never had a family and grew up in what orphanage?

Q648. In one of the most emotional episodes of any series, Cherry White, the sweet Red Cross nurse who volunteered for duty in Nam, was killed in a bombing before she could accomplish her greatest desire. What was it?

CHiPs
NBC, 1977–83

Q649. Ponch Poncherello and Jon Baker were members of CHiPs, the California Highway Patrol. What brand of motorcycle did the officers ride?

Q650. Officer Bonnie Clark took sign communication at Cal State and was now a part of the Deaf Liaison Program. What nickname did Ponch have for her?

A642. $100.

A643. Karen Colosky

A644. "Never seen an outie before?"

A645. The rain

A646. "K.C. from K.C."

A647. Lady of Perpetual Hope

A648. To find her brother Rick, who was reported as missing in action

CHiPs

A649. Kawasaki

A650. "Bon Bon"

CHiPs continued

Q651. The police department attempted to introduce efficiency in CHiPs via a robotics program. What was the program called?

Civil Wars
ABC, 1991–93

Q652. Sydney Guilford, Charlie Howell, and Eli Levinson were three friends who operated a law firm in New York City that handled divorces. What was their retainer and what was their hourly rate?

Q653. Denise Ianello, the firm's pretty but sometimes far-out legal secretary, was born in New York, went to P.S. 147 grammar school, and Sacred Heart High School. What secretarial school did she attend?

Columbo
NBC/ABC, 1971–91

Q654. Lieutenant Columbo is famous for his rumpled raincoat and pretense of muddleheadedness. He felt there was something wrong with him "because I seem to bother people and make them nervous." The viewer knew Columbo was closing in on a culprit when he uttered his famous catchphrase. What is it?

Q655. Columbo enjoyed his coffee hot, strong, and black, drove a battered Peugeot, and had two dogs. The first one (when the series was on NBC) was Fang. When the series switched to ABC (1989–91) what did Columbo call the dog?

Q656. Columbo smoked cigars but his never-seen wife preferred pipes if he must smoke. Why wouldn't Columbo smoke a pipe?

A651. MERV (Maximum Efficiency Robotization, Vector Section 1)

Civil Wars

A652. $7,500 retainer; $300 an hour

A653. The Kathie Gibbs School

Columbo

A654. "Oh, one more thing."

A655. "Dog. He's a dog so we call him dog."

A656. "It's too much for me to carry around."

The Commish
ABC, 1990–

Q657. Tony Scali, the chief of the Eastbridge Police Department, is affectionately called "The Commish." He was born in Brooklyn and attended St. Mary's High School. From what real college did Tony get his law degree?

Q658. Tony dreams of becoming the police commissioner and is studying to do just that. In the opening theme Tony is seen reading a book. What book is it?

Q659. Tony's loving wife, Rachel, is a teacher—at what school?

Dark Shadows
ABC, 1966–71

Q660. Victoria Winters was a young woman who came to the fishing village of Collinsport to become the tutor to nine-year-old David Collins, who lived with his father, Roger; Roger's sister, Elizabeth; and Elizabeth's daughter, Carolyn. The family owned the town and resided in what mansion on the Collinswood Estates?

Q661. Victoria soon discovered the supernatural to be present on the estate. She was helped at times by the spirit of Josette Collins, who killed herself a century earlier by jumping off a forbidding cliff overlooking the ocean. What was this area called?

Q662. When Josette appeared, there was no mistaking her presence. Her portrait glowed and the scent of her perfume was evident. What scent was it?

Q663. Barnabas Collins was a 175-year-old vampire who was set free by Willie Loomis when seeking the jewels that were supposedly buried with Barnabas. Barnabas was concealed in a secret room in the family crypt. Where is the crypt located?

The Commish

A657. Fordham University in the Bronx

A658. *Tissue Decomposition: A Homicide Primer*

A659. The Eastbridge Grammar School

Dark Shadows

A660. The Great House

A661. Widow's Hill

A662. Jasmine

A663. Eagle Hill Cemetery

Doogie Howser, M.D.
ABC, 1989–93

Q664. Sixteen-year-old Doogie Howser was not a normal teen-ager; he was a genius and a doctor with the Eastman Medical Center. When Doogie wanted to see if he could become just another teen, he took a part-time job at what fast-food emporium?

Q665. Doogie's friend, Vinnie, was a budding film director hoping to get into California's Institute of the Arts. In an attempt to impress a producer, Vinnie wrote a movie script called what?

Q666. At the end of each episode Doogie was seen entering the day's activities into his computer. What did he call these notes?

The Dukes of Hazzard
CBS, 1979–85

Q667. Jefferson Davis Hogg, the corrupt "Boss" of rural Hazzard County, Georgia, attempted to control the town but was continually foiled by the Dukes, a peace-loving clan who felt it was their duty to right wrongs. Uncle Jesse was the head of the family and he ran a farm with nephews Bo and Luke and niece Daisy. What was the location of the Duke farm?

Q668. "The law is the law and we Dukes gotta obey it no matter what," says Uncle Jesse. But at one point Jesse was a lawbreaker. What did he do?

Q669. Bo and Luke had a souped-up 1969 Dodge Charger called the General Lee. The car had the racing number 1 on its sides. What was on the roof?

Q670. Daisy's mode of transportation was not as fancy as Bo or Luke's: she drove a jeep. What did she call it?

Q671. Sheriff Roscoe P. Coltrane was Boss Hogg's corrupt assistant. He had office number 101 and patrolled the streets with his bloodhound. What was the dog's name?

Doogie Howser, M.D.

A664.   Burger Baby

A665.   *The Black Lizard*

A666.   "The Personal Journal of Doogie Howser, M.D."

The Dukes of Hazzard

A667.   Old Mill Road

A668.   Ran moonshine from his stills

A669.   The Confederate flag

A670.   Dixie

A671.   Flash

Dynasty
ABC, 1981–89

Wealthy Blake Carrington was married to Krystle. He owned a mansion at 173 Essex Drive in Denver, Colorado, and ran the Denver-Carrington Oil Company. Name the businesses of these other *Dynasty* regulars:

Q672. Alexis Carrington Colby, Blake's ex-wife, owns what oil company?

Q673. Blake's daughter, Fallon, runs what hotel?

Q674. Sammy Jo Dean, Krystle's niece, operates what stables?

Q675. The woman of mystery, Dominque Devereaux, owns what record company?

Eight Is Enough
ABC, 1977–81

Q676. The Bradfords were a ten-member family who lived in Sacramento. Tom was married to Abby, his second wife, but had eight children by his first wife, Joanie. David, the oldest son, was a contractor and formed the Bradford Construction Company with Tom. For what company did David work before starting his own business?

Q677. Family friend Dr. Craig Maxwell was oldest daughter Mary Bradford's inspiration to become a doctor. At what hospital did Mary intern?

Q678. Joanie was named after her mother and had her mother's eyes, smile, and sensitivity. She was first a researcher, then a reporter, for what TV station?

Q679. Nancy was the prettiest of the Bradford girls. Before acquiring a job at a brokerage house, Nancy worked as a model in TV commercials. What product did she represent?

Q680. Susan, the most sensitive of the girls and the most indecisive about her future, eventually found her calling operating a day care center. She was also the second child to wed (David was first), marrying Merle Stockwell, a ballplayer for what team?

Dynasty

A672. Colbyco

A673. LaMirage

A674. Delta Rho

A675. Titiana

Eight Is Enough

A676. Mann Construction

A677. St. Mary's

A678. KTNS, Channel 8

A679. She was the Sunshine Soda Girl.

A680. The Cyclones

Eight Is Enough continued

Q681. Tommy was the most troublesome of the Bradford children. He was rebellious and wanted to quit school to become a rock musician. Name the band he started.

Q682. Elizabeth and Nicholas were the youngest kids. Elizabeth had aspirations to become a dancer. Nicholas was in grammar school and had two pet hamsters. What were their names?

The Fall Guy
ABC, 1981–86

Q683. "I'm not the kind to kiss and tell but I've been seen with Farrah...I've gotten burned over Cheryl Tiegs, blown up for Raquel Welch...I'm the unknown stuntman who makes Eastwood look so fine..." So said the theme as it described Colt Seavers, a movie and TV stuntman for what organization?

Q684. Colt was also a bounty hunter for the Los Angeles Criminal Courts System. He worked for several different bailbondsmen, but what did he carry as a weapon "to impress people"?

Q685. Living in a cabin in the woods that was somewhat off the beaten path, Colt found that soaking in his outdoor tub relaxed him. He also had a favorite watering hole. What was it?

Q686. Samantha Jack, Teri Michaels, and Pearl Sperling were the bailbonds"men" who hired Colt to track down criminals. What company did the women represent?

Q687. Colt's cousin, Howie Munson, was a budding stuntman who worked as Colt's business manager. What did Colt call Howie?

A681.   Tommy and the Actions

A682.   Ron and Marsha

The Fall Guy

A683.   Fall Guy Stunt Association

A684.   A movie stuntgun with three-quarter-load blanks

A685.   The Palomino Club

A686.   Bond Street Bail

A687.   "Kid"

Family
ABC, 1976–80

Q688. The Lawrences were a middle-income family of six living in Pasadena. Doug, a lawyer, and his wife, Kate, were the parents of Nancy, Willie, Buddy and Annie. At the start of the second season Quinn Cummings joined the cast as Annie Cooper, an eleven-year-old who came to live with the Lawrences when her parents were killed in a car accident. What were her parents' first names?

Q689. Doug and Kate's oldest, Nancy, was attending law school, while middle child Willie worked for a TV game show that was a takeoff on *The Dating Game*. What was it called?

Q690. Buddy, whose real name is Letitia, was the "baby" of the family. She and Annie attended the same school. Name it.

Fantasy Island
ABC, 1978–84

Q691. "Da plane, da plane." These words, spoken by diminutive Tattoo, indicated that guests were arriving on Fantasy Island to have their dreams granted by Mr. Roarke, the mysterious owner of the place. Mr. Roarke appeared to be an immortal (he was over three hundred years old) and for centuries had been battling what evil?

Q692. Fantasy Island was, of course, totally surrounded by water, in which lived many strange creatures. It was known, for example, that a mermaid called these waters home. Michelle Phillips played the role. What was her name?

Family

A688. Grace and Ralph

A689. *The Dame Game*

A690. Quenton Junior High

Fantasy Island

A691. The Devil

A692. Princess Nyah

Father Dowling Mysteries
NBC/ABC, 1989–91

Q693. Father Dowling and Sister Steve, a novice nun, were amateur detectives who helped the police solve crimes. Father Dowling had been pastor at St. Michael's parish for nine years and was a Chicago Cubs fan. Sherlock Holmes was his hero and he was an avid mystery book and magazine reader. What is his favorite magazine?

Q694. Father Dowling first met Stevie at F.W. Woolworth. She was a juvie and he caught her shoplifting. Under his guidance her life was turned around. When she received her confirmation, Stevie took an unusual middle name. What was it?

Q695. Sister Steve loved to visit the zoo. When she was a kid she befriended a monkey that to this day looked forward to seeing her. What did she name the monkey?

Q696. When a TV producer read of Father Dowling's exploits in the local newspaper, he came to Chicago to make a series based on the priest's adventures. What was the series to be called?

The Flash
CBS, 1990–91

Q697. Before Barry Allen became the Flash, a crimefighter in Central City in 1990, there had been another champion of the underdog. He rode in a black car, wore a black costume, and used "Tranq bullets." Who was he?

Q698. Barry Allen turned into the Flash when he was accidentally dowsed with chemicals. His assistant was Tina McGee, a government scientist who helped him establish his Flash alias. For what agency did Tina work?

Q699. The Flash was capable of fantastic speeds and required much food to maintain his strength. Tina had calculated how fast Barry could run; in fact he could cause sonic booms. Just what was Barry's speed?

Father Dowling Mysteries

A693. *Armchair Sleuth*

A694. Sivle (Elvis spelled backwards)

A695. Diogenes

A696. *Father Flaherty Investigates*

The Flash

A697. The Night Shade

A698. Star Labs

A699. 620 mph

Fly by Night
CBS, 1990–92

Q700. Slick Air was a one-plane airline owned by Sally Monroe that could handle thirty passengers. What kind of plane did Sally own?

Q701. The Federal Trade Development Bank held the mortgage on Slick Air. Sally's business was based at the Ellis Airport and she lived nearby in Vancouver. What was Sally's favorite watering hole?

The Greatest American Hero
ABC, 1981–83

Q702. To prevent Earth from destroying itself, aliens from an unknown planet chose two earthlings to wage a war on crime: Ralph Hinkley, a schoolteacher, and Bill Maxwell, an FBI agent. The aliens selected Ralph to become the Greatest American Hero because he possessed three qualities. Name them.

Q703. The aliens gave Ralph a costume that endowed him with special powers. Ralph called it "the suit." What was Bill's name for it?

Q704. While Ralph did try to keep his newfound abilities a secret, many people witnessed his amazing feats. What newspaper was first to publish a picture of Ralph flying?

Q705. Bill referred to the aliens as "the little green guys" and sometimes has a difficult time explaining to his superiors how he managed to crack a case without involving Ralph. To relax himself, Bill enjoyed snacking on what something most people would not eat?

Fly by Night

A700.   B-27

A701.   The Bomber's Bar

The Greatest American Hero

A702.   A strong moral character, integrity, and a healthy idealism

A703.   "The Jammies"

A704.   *The Daily Galaxy*

A705.   Dog biscuits

Hardcastle and McCormick
ABC, 1983–86

Q706. Milton C. Hardcastle was a judge known for his harsh courtroom sentences and Mark McCormick was a two-time loser up for his third offense. To avoid a prison term, Mark joined the judge in an effort to bring to justice the criminals who were tried but were set free by technicalities. The judge had a nickname that he received while serving on the bench. What was it?

Q707. Mark also had a nickname, but his was associated with stealing cars. He was not known for his driving skills and the nickname reflected it. What was it?

Hart to Hart
ABC, 1979–84

Q708. Jennifer and Jonathan Hart were a wealthy couple who helped people in trouble. Jonathan, the owner of Hart Industries, and Jennifer, a former journalist, met in London, married, and honeymooned in California's Napa Valley. They stayed in room 7 of what inn?

Q709. Jennifer was born in Hillhaven, Maryland, and attended the Gresham Prep School. At that time she also had a favorite horse on her father's ranch. What did she call the horse?

Q710. Jennifer tended to get a little tipsy from champagne and frequently lunched at La Scala's Restaurant. She also played a party hostess on what favorite daytime TV drama?

Hawaiian Eye
ABC, 1959–63

Q711. Tracy Steele, Tom Lopaka, and Gregg MacKenzie were private detectives called "The Eyes," a shortened name for their company. What was the exact name of their firm?

Q712. The Eyes operated from the Hilton Hawaiian Village Hotel where their friend and sometimes assistant, Cricket Blake, worked. Cricket ran the gift shop in the hotel. What was her business called?

Hardcastle and McCormick

A706. "Hardcase"

A707. "Skid"

Hart to Hart

A708. The O'Berge Inn

A709. Sweet Sue

A710. *Doctors' Hospital*

Hawaiian Eye

A711. Hawaiian Eye—Investigation-Protection

A712. Cricket's Corner

Hawaiian Eye continued

Q713. In addition to the gift shop, Cricket also earned money as a singer at the hotel. In what room did Cricket perform?

Q714. Each of the detectives had an eye for beautiful women and Tom and Tracy had a special nickname for Cricket. What did they call her?

In the Heat of the Night
NBC/CBS, 1988–

Q715. Bill Gillespie is the white police chief of Sparta, Mississippi, and Virgil Tibbs is his black chief of detectives. Tibbs is married to Aletha, a schoolteacher; Gillespie is a widower who, before he began romancing Harriet DeLong, a black city councilwoman, dated JoAnn St. John, a former prostitute who was trying to turn her life around. JoAnn worked at Gillespie's favorite eatery. What was it?

Q716. Gillespie enjoys hunting in his spare time and sometimes rides with his hunting dog in his patrol car. What is the dog's name?

Q717. Parker Williams is one of Gillespie's deputies. He has three cats and his favorite watering hole is the Big T Truck Stop. Name at least two of his cats.

The Invaders
ABC, 1967–68

Q718. The aliens (called Invaders) are here; one man, David Vincent, has seen them. Could he convince a disbelieving world that the nightmare had already begun? Returning home from a business trip late one night and getting tired, David had taken an exit off Highway 166 and found himself on a desolate country road. It was here that David had his close encounter. At what time of morning did this happen?

A713.   The Shell Lounge

A714.   "Lover"

In the Heat of the Night

A715.   The Magnolia Cafe

A716.   Roscoe

A717.   Old Man, Fuzz Face, Wrencher

The Invaders

A718.   4:20

The Invaders continued

Q719. The Invaders had taken human form and planned to assimilate into society. Their transformations were not always perfect and David knew their one flaw. What was it?

Q720. The Invaders were emotionless in any form, but some aliens developed emotions. What did the alien leaders call these outcasts?

The Islanders
ABC, 1960–61

Q721. Sandy Wade and Zack Malloy ran a small airline on an island in Sumatra. What was the name of this island ("whose chief natural resources are beautiful native girls")?

Q722. Argumentative partners Sandy and Zack were brought together by a mutual lady friend, Willie Vandeveer. Feeling both were going nowhere and needed a business, she was now their treasurer. Malloy and Company and Southern Cross were two of the names the trio rejected for their airline. What did they finally agree on for a name?

Q723. Shipwreck Callahan's was the American bar on the island. Shipwreck Callahan was the owner and the bank of Jakarta held the mortgage on the bar. What was Callahan's favorite drink to serve?

Jake and the Fatman
CBS, 1987–92

Q724. J.L. McCabe was first a district attorney, then a prosecuting attorney. J.L. was grossly overweight and had a similarly overweight dog named Max. McCabe had two nicknames; one of them was the "Fatman." What was the other?

Q725. J.L. was assisted by Jake Styles and Neely Capshaw. As a kid Jake had the nickname "Butchie," and the mythical Tom Cody was the star of his favorite TV show. What was it?

A719. "Some of them have mutated hands; a crooked fourth finger."

A720. Mutants

The Islanders

A721. Ambowina

A722. Lato Airways

A723. A bamboo bomb

Jake and the Fatman

A724. "Buster"

A725. *Sky Hawk*

Johnny Bago
CBS, 1993

Q726. Johnny Tenuti was on the run from the mob for whacking a godfather's son. Though innocent, Johnny couldn't prove it unless he could find the real killer, a tattooed woman. He used the alias Johnny Bago and roamed the country in a Winnebago seeking to clear his name with the boys. What was the unique nameplate on the back of the bago?

Q727. Johnny had become a news item and had been featured on a TV reality show as a wanted criminal. What TV show had criminal profiles of him?

Q728. Beverly Florio was Johnny's ex-wife, a parole officer who was also after Johnny. She drove a beatup N.Y.P.D. station wagon and hoped to get Johnny before the mob did. The police car she drove was registered to what unit of the department?

Key West
Fox, 1993

Q729. After hitting a million-dollar lotto, Seamus O'Neill quit his job and moved to Key West to live like his hero, Ernest Hemingway. His joy was short lived when he got his first lotto check. How much was it for?

Q730. King Cole was Seamus's boss, the editor of the town's only newspaper. What was the name of the paper?

Q731. Gumbo owned the local hangout and had an alligator who "dreams of devouring a beautiful native girl who is helplessly tied to a tree." What had Gumbo named the alligator?

Q732. Savanagh was the local prostitute. She was proud to sell her body for money ("It was a lifelong dream of mine since childhood") and charged how much a night?

Johnny Bago

A726. Travelin' Timberdoodle

A727. *America at Large*

A728. K-9 Squad

Key West

A729. $32.59

A730. *The Meteor*

A731. Tickled Pink

A732. $1,000

Knight Rider
NBC, 1982–86

Q733. KITT, the Knight Industries 2000, was a sleek car specially designed to battle crime. It could speak, had been programmed to protect human life, and was virtually indestructible. KITT could travel over any substance, even water. What system allowed this?

Q734. Being a car did limit KITT to where it could go. When neither Michael Knight, its driver, nor KITT could get into an area that needed investigating, what device did Michael use?

Q735. Before Wilton Knight perfected KITT, he produced KARR, an evil prototype that had no respect for human life. What did KARR stand for?

Life Goes On
ABC, 1989–93

Q736. The Thatchers were a Catholic family of five (Drew and Libby were the parents; Paige, Becca, and Corky their children), residing in the town of Glen Brook. Drew was a construction worker who quit his job for a better opportunity—to own his own business, a diner. For what construction company had he worked?

Q737. Libby was a singer and dancer who gave up her career to raise a family. She starred, for example, in an Off-Broadway production of *West Side Story*. What was her stage name at the time?

Q738. Libby was now with the Berkson and Berkson Ad Agency and, since going back to work, missed her favorite TV soap opera. What show was it?

Q739. Paige, Drew's somewhat rebellious daughter from a first marriage, was undecided about her future until she and a friend began their own construction company. What was the name of their business?

Knight Rider

A733.   A third-stage aquatic synthesizer

A734.   SID (Satellite Infiltration Drone)

A735.   Knight Automated Roving Robot

Life Goes On

A736.   Quentico

A737.   Libby Dean

A738.   *Forever and a Day*

A739.   Darlin' Construction Company

Life Goes On continued

Q740. Becca was fifteen and a talented ballerina who hoped to one day become a writer. Because she had a tendency to write articles that are considered too controversial for her school newspaper at Marshall High, she turned to the school's forbidden tabloid. Name this paper.

Q741. Corky, afflicted with Down's syndrome, tried to be like other kids. Before attending Marshall High School, Corky was enrolled in an institution to help him function. What was the name of the school?

The Love Boat
ABC, 1977–87

Q742. The *Pacific Princess* was a luxury cruise ship that had been nicknamed "The Love Boat" by her crew. What company owned the ship?

Q743. Before it became the *Pacific Princess*, the ship was called the *Sun Princess* in the 1976 pilot film. In honor of the show's 1,000th guest star, the ship's name was changed once again. Name either the 1,000th guest or the ship's new moniker.

McMillan and Wife
NBC, 1971–76

Q744. When Sally, the wife of San Francisco Police Commissioner Stewart McMillan, began courses in gourmet cooking, she prepared meals Mac "loved." Name at least one of these gourmet meals.

Q745. Mildred was the McMillans' housekeeper. She called herself by a specific name. What was it?

Magnum, P.I.
CBS, 1980–88

Q746. Thomas Magnum, a former naval intelligence officer turned private detective, lived on the estate of pulp writer Robin Masters in return for providing its security. As a P.I., how much a day did Magnum charge?

A740. *The Underground Marshall*

A741. The Fowler Institute

The Love Boat

A742. Pacific Cruise Lines

A743. Lana Turner or the *Royal Princess*

McMillan and Wife

A744. Rattlesnake béarnaise or walnut casserole in goat butter

A745. "A Jack of all trades in the McMillan household."

Magnum, P.I.

A746. $200

Magnum, P.I. *continued*

Q747. Magnum was born in the town of Tidewater, Virginia, and had his first job delivering newspapers for the *Daily Sentinel*. What did Magnum earn a week at the time?

Q748. Magnum recorded his experiences as a detective, hoping to one day turn his notes into a book. He regularly mentioned what he was going to call the book. What was it?

Q749. Jonathan Higgins, the estate's major domo, was a survival expert with endless stories about his experiences during the war. Higgins had two dogs who helped him patrol the estate, Zeus and Apollo. By what nickname were they called?

Q750. Robin Masters was never seen. Higgins acted on Robin's behalf and Magnum suspected that Higgins was Robin but he couldn't prove it. What was the common nickname for Masters' estate?

Q751. T.C. and Rick were Magnum's friends, who served with him in Vietnam. Rick tended bar and T.C. ran a helicopter charter service. What was the name of T.C.'s company?

Matlock
NBC/ABC, 1986–

Q752. Ben Matlock is a rumpled Atlanta-based lawyer who has a record of successfully defending clients. He is also known for his high prices. How much does it cost to hire Ben?

Q753. Ben snacks on hot dogs at every opportunity and prefers to "wash it down" with soda. What flavor of soda does Ben drink?

Q754. Ben doesn't trust police labs and prefers to do his own investigating. What has he against police labs?

Q755. Ben rises every morning at five ("It's the best time for thinking") and is very strict about one thing which he prohibits in his office (and that even applies to his best-paying clients). What is it?

A747.　$12 plus a penny for each paper sold

A748.　"How to Be a World Class Private Investigator."

A749.　"The Lads"

A750.　"Robin's Nest"

A751.　Island Hoppers

Matlock

A752.　$100,000

A753.　Grape

A754.　"They're not working for my client."

A755.　Smoking

Max Headroom
ABC, 1987

Q756. In a future time, Network 23 was the top-rated TV station. Channel switching during commercials had become a major problem because it caused a dip in Network 23's ratings. There were a number of competing TV stations; name at least two.

Q757. Overweight or inactive people built up electrical charges; active people burned these charges off. To prevent channel switching, Network 23 began airing subliminal commercials that compressed thirty seconds into only three. These commercials violently stimulated the electrical charges in overweight and inactive people and caused them to explode (spontaneously combust). What were these commercials called?

Q758. Network 23 broadcasts via the Comstat 2058 Satellite. What was the network's slogan?

Melrose Place
Fox, 1991–

Q759. Young singles in an apartment complex at 4616 Melrose Place provide the setting. What is the local watering hole?

Q760. Sandy is an aspiring actress who had her first role in an unnamed horror flick. How does she describe her film debut?

Q761. Jane, a budding fashion designer, runs a small boutique. What is its name?

Midnight Caller
NBC, 1988–91

Q762. Jack Kilian was a former police inspector now hosting a radio call-in program, *Midnight Caller*. On what station did the show air?

Q763. The telephone number of the radio station was 555-TALK and it was located at 93.3 on the FM dial. By what name did Jack call himself on the air?

Max Headroom

A756. BBC 126, Planet Wide, Big Time TV, Channel 1111, PornoVision, Channel 28, Rubbish TV

A757. Blipverts

A758. "The Network That Means Business"

Melrose Place

A759. Shooters (a bar-poolroom)

A760. "Eight lines, two screams, and a topless scene."

A761. The Mart

Midnight Caller

A762. KCJM

A763. "The Nighthawk"

Moonlighting
ABC, 1985–89

Q764. Maddie Hayes was a model left penniless when her business manager embezzled her funds. Before she was able to sell a failed detective agency, one of her holdings, to raise money, David Addison talked her into saving it. She changed the name of the agency to Blue Moon Investigations and became a private detective. What was the agency's original name?

Q765. Maddie had appeared on the covers of such magazines as *Vogue* and *Glamour* and represented what product on TV?

Q766. "Do bears bear? Do bees bee?" was David's catchphrase. He also said that he is a capitalist ("I take my capital wherever I can get it"). David had an alliterative nickname for Maddie. What was it?

Murder, She Wrote
CBS, 1984–

Q767. Jessica Fletcher is a successful mystery author whose books include *All Fall Down Dead, The Corpse Wasn't There,* and *The Killer Called Collect*. What was the title of her very first book?

Q768. Jessica was a former English teacher whose late husband was named Frank. A central feature of her mysteries is a Saint-like character. Name him.

Q769. Living mainly in the small town of Cabot Cove, Maine, Jessica has two passions. One is riding her bicycle around town; what is the other?

Q770. When she is not in Maine, Jessica can be found in New York City, where she has an apartment at the Penfield House. She took the apartment to be near her publisher and to teach criminology at what college?

Moonlighting

A764. City of Angels Investigations

A765. Blue Moon Shampoo

A766. "Blondie Blonde"

Murder, She Wrote

A767. *The Corpse Danced at Midnight*

A768. Damian Sinclair

A769. Fishing

A770. Manhattan University

Naked City
ABC, 1958–63

Q77I. "There are eight million stories in the Naked City. This has been one of them." These spoken words ended each episode with perhaps the most famous line in TV history. The Naked City was Manhattan, and programs were character studies of the people of a large metropolis. The police detectives of what New York City precinct were featured on the program?

Q772. Today, the New York City Police Department is known by the initials N.Y.P.D. But, on the series, different initials appeared on police vehicles. What were they?

Northern Exposure
CBS, 1990–

Q773. Joel Fleischman is a misplaced medical school graduate who began his practice in Cicely, Alaska, a small town that bankrolled his studies. Joel attended Camp Indian Head as a kid, went to Richfield High School, and graduated from Columbia University Medical School. At what hospital did he do his internship?

Q774. Cicely has a population of 215 (counting Joel) and has an elevation of 6,572 feet. There has never been a doctor's office in Cicely, so Joel was given an abandoned building for his practice. What occupied the place before Joel?

Q775. Maggie O'Connell is Joel's landlady. She was born in Michigan and now owns a one-plane company. What is it called?

Q776. Cicely is virtually crime free. However, during the spring thaw, when the ice breaks, "people go crazy." What happens?

Q777. Maurice Minifield, a former NASA astronaut, founded the town of Cicely. The local paper is the Cicely *World Telegram* and Minifield Communications runs the only radio station. What is its nickname?

Naked City

A771.   65th

A772.   P.D.N.Y.C. (Police Department of New York City)

Northern Exposure

A773.   Beth Sinai

A774.   Northwestern Mining

A775.   O'Connell Air Taxi Service

A776.   They steal things.

A777.   "Great Bear Radio"

Perry Mason
CBS, 1957–63

Q778. Erle Stanley Gardner's brilliant criminal attorney, Perry Mason, came to TV in 1957. To contact Perry by phone, one simply called Hollywood 2-1799. If you wanted to meet with Mr. Mason, where would you find his office?

Q779. Perry seemed to be "all work and no play" but he did enjoy eating at what particular diner in Los Angeles?

Q780. While rarely seen consulting a law book, Perry did have a library, which was shown under the closing credits. Name one of the two books seen.

Picket Fences
CBS, 1992–

Q781. Rome, Wisconsin, seems like a charming little town, but behind its picket fences lie many strange things. Jimmy Brock is its sheriff and Max Stewart and Kenny Lacos are his deputies. Max is a beautiful brunette who doesn't seem like the type to kill, but when it comes to upholding the law, she will do what it takes. Name the two murderers she is famous for gunning down.

Q782. Jimmy is married to Jill and is the father of three children, Kimberly, Matthew, and Zachary. Jill is a private-practice doctor who is also on call where?

Q783. The *Herald* is the town's newspaper; Douglas Wambaugh is the outlandish defense attorney; and Henry Bone is the town's only judge. In what county are cases tried?

Police Woman
NBC, 1974–78

Q784. Pepper Anderson was a glamorous fashion model who, bored with her career, became a police officer to find more excitement in life. With what division of the L.A.P.D. did Pepper work?

Perry Mason

A778. Suite 904 in the Brent Building in Los Angeles

A779. McQuade's Bar and Grill

A780. *Corpus Juris*, Vol. 39 and Vol. 51

Picket Fences

A781. The Green Bay Chopper and the Cupid Killer

A782. Norwood Hospital

A783. Hogan County

Police Woman

A784. Criminal Conspiracy Division

Police Woman continued

Q785. When Pepper first joined the force, she was assigned to undercover work of a different kind. It was kind of tacky and Pepper didn't really like it. What job was it?

Q786. Pepper was a nickname and, although it was rarely mentioned, she did have a real first name. What was it?

Reasonable Doubts
NBC, 1991–93

Q787. Richard "Dicky" Cobb was a tough detective who is assigned by the D.A.'s office to assist Tess Kaufman, a hearing-impaired prosecuting attorney. Although knowing sign language, Cobb did not attend school to learn it. How did he learn sign?

Q788. Cobb's romantic interest was Kay Lockman, the owner of his favorite bar. Name this watering hole.

Remington Steele
NBC, 1982–86

Q789. Remington Steele did not actually exist. He was created by private investigator Laura Holt as "front man" to save her faltering business. An unknown thief crossed her path and to get out of a scrape, posed as Remington Steele. He later talked Laura into making him her partner. Before beginning her own business (Laura Holt Investigations), she was employed by what outfit?

Q790. As a kid Laura had the nickname "Binky," and *Atomic Man* was her favorite TV show. And, since a youngster "the Holt Curse" had followed her into adulthood. What was "the Holt Curse?"

Q791. Remington was a movie and TV fan and solved crimes based on old movie plots. When taking cases, Remington assumed names all taken from the films of his favorite actor. Who was it?

A785.   Detective with the vice squad

A786.   Lee Anne (but also mentioned as Suzanne)

Reasonable Doubts

A787.   From his deaf father

A788.   The Set Up Bar

Remington Steele

A789.   Havenhurst Detective Agency

A790.   A craving for chocolate that is difficult to control

A791.   Humphrey Bogart

Remington Steele continued

Q792. The man who took the name of Remington Steele was born in Ireland and was apparently an orphan. He was taken in by a sophisticated thief and taught the fine art of crime. Who took Remington under his wing?

Richard Diamond, Private Detective
CBS/NBC, 1957–60

Q793. "A detective is only as good as his snitch," was the motto of Richard Diamond, a rugged private eye working out of New York City. How much did Diamond pay his snitches?

Q794. Richard called her "Samuel" and he had never seen her. She was Diamond's telephone answering service girl. What is the name of the company she ran?

Q795. The viewer had a slight advantage over Diamond in that a bit of Sam, mostly her very shapely legs, could be seen. First Mary Tyler Moore, then Roxanne Brooks played the role. What size stockings did "Samuel" wear?

The Roaring 20's
ABC, 1960–62

Q796. The Charleston Club on East 52nd Street was a hot nightspot owned by Pinky Pinkham and frequented by newspaper reporters Pat Garrison and Scott Norris. Pinky was also a singer at the club and she rarely used her real first name. What was it?

Q797. Scott and Pat were reporters who often played detective to get a story. What was their salary when the series began?

Q798. Scott and Pat worked for the *Record* and their favorite bar was located next to the Record Building. What was it called?

A792.   Daniel Chalmers

Richard Diamond, Private Detective

A793. $10

A794.   The Hi-Fi Answering Service

A795.   Size 10 medium length

The Roaring 20's

A796.   Delaware

A797. $40

A798.   Chauncey's

Search
NBC, 1972–73

Q799. Probe was a supercomputerized detective agency specializing in the recovery of whatever is missing ("If you lose it, we find it"). Based in Washington, D.C., Probe operated out of what organization?

Q800. Hugh Lockwood, Nick Bianco, and Chris Grover were three highly skilled investigators who worked for Probe. Hugh's code was Probe One. What were the code names for Nick and Chris?

Q801. Each agent had a superminiaturized transmitter/receiver surgically implanted in the ear. What was this device called?

Q802. Sensing devices were implanted in agent's bodies and a body detector under their skin. Each agent also carried an ultraminiaturized TV camera capable of transmitting from any part of the world. How was the signal picked up by Probe Control?

77 Sunset Strip
ABC, 1958–64

Q803. 77 Sunset Strip was the business address of private detectives Stu Bailey and Jeff Spencer. Girls often said, "You're too cute to be a snoop," when they saw Jeff, who read *Playboy* magazine and was quite generous to his snitches. How much did he pay them?

Q804. Dino's Lodge was located next to 77 Sunset Strip and Gerald Lloyd Kookson III, a.k.a. Kookie, was its parking lot attendant. Kookie drove a hot rod and used hip (for the time) terms like "Squaresville, Man." He also had what slang term for Stu and Jeff?

Q805. Kookie had a flamboyant way of combing his hair that drove teenage girls crazy. Trouble was "Troublesville" and he had a term for pretty chicks. What was it?

Q806. Suzanne Fabray worked the switchboard in office 103 at 77 Sunset Strip. What was the name of her company?

Search

A799. World Securities Corporation

A800. Nick was Omega Probe; Chris was Standby Probe.

A801. An Ear Check

A802. By Tele Communications Transatlantic Net via Tracking Station Niner Six Grid

77 Sunset Strip

A803. $50

A804. "Hey, Dad"

A805. "Dreamboats"

A806. The Sunset Answering Service

77 Sunset Strip continued

Q807. Dino's Lodge closed at two in the morning, and the Frankie Ortega Trio provided the supper club's music. Dino also had a business in the back of the lodge that catered to the pampered dogs of its patrons. What was it called?

Silk Stalkings
CBS, 1991–

Q808. Rita Lee Lance and Chris Lorenzo are Florida police detectives who investigate society murders they call "Silk Stalkings." For what area of the Palm Springs Police Department do Rita and Chris work?

Q809. Rita and Chris's favorite sport is golf, and golfing great Sammy Snead is their hero. By what nickname do Rita and Chris call each other?

Sisters
NBC, 1991–

Q810. The lives of four close-knit sisters (Georgie, Teddy, Alex, and Frankie) are depicted on a weekly basis. All the sisters have male names. Why?

Q811. Their lives were made into a TV movie with the premise "Four sisters for each other forever." What was the movie called?

Q812. Georgie has a Ph.D. in anthropology but works as a real estate broker for what company?

Q813. Alex is the tight-fisted one of the family and was married to Wade until he left her for a younger woman. What leisure- time activity did Wade enjoy?

Q814. Teddy is the unstable sister and has held a number of jobs. She is a budding artist and fashion designer whose most famous client was First Lady Hillary Clinton. For what department store did Teddy design clothes?

A807.   Dino's Poodle Palace

Silk Stalkings

A808.   The Crimes of Passion Unit

A809.   "Sam"

Sisters

A810.   Their father had hoped for boys.

A811.   *A Sister's Love*

A812.   Maple Leaf Realties

A813.   Dressing in women's clothes

A814.   Bolzak's

Sisters continued

Q815. Frankie, the youngest of the four, is closest to Teddy. What nickname for Frankie as a youngster does Teddy still use?

South Beach
NBC, 1993

Q816. "I don't come cheap or easy," said Kate Patrick, a beautiful thief who worked for Roberts, a government agent who used criminals (like Kate) for undercover assignments. Kate was proud of her collection of exotic fish. What was the rarest fish she had in her aquarium?

Q817. Roxie, who dressed in various outfits and was called "Chameleon," operated a hotel for Roberts where Kate lives. What was its name?

Street Hawk
ABC, 1985

Q818. Operation Street Hawk was a top-secret project concerned with law enforcement. It was basically an attack motorcycle being tested by local police departments. Norman Tuttle created Street Hawk and Jesse Mach was his test pilot. Norman had added four high-volume air boxes and hyperthrust. Street Hawk normally cruised at 200 mph. What was its maximum speed?

Q819. Norman's dream was to see Street Hawk in every police department. He was also very protective of the bike and cringed at times at the way Jesse mishandled her. What "term of endearment" did Norman have for Street Hawk?

SurfSide 6
ABC, 1960–62

Q820. SurfSide 6 was a houseboat and the address of a detective agency owned by Dave Thorne, Sandy Winfield, and Ken Madison. Where in Miami Beach is the houseboat docked?

A815. "Stinkerbelle"

South Beach

A816. A Blue Phantom

A817. The Red Sands Hotel

Street Hawk

A818. 300 mph

A819. "My Baby"

SurfSide 6

A820. At Indian Creek

SurfSide 6 continued

Q821. Daphne DeWitt Dutton, who lived on the neighboring yacht, was a beautiful jet setter and heir to the Dutton Racing Stables. What did she name the horse at the stables that she raised from a colt?

Q822. Cha Cha O'Brien was the club singer at the Fontaine-bleau Hotel, located opposite SurfSide 6 on Ocean Avenue. In what room did she perform?

The Waltons
CBS, 1972–81

Q823. Waltons Mountain in the Blue Ridge Mountains of Virginia was not owned by the Walton family ("we sort of hold it in trust"). What ancestor settled on the mountain in 1789?

Q824. John and Olivia were the parents of six children and lived in Jefferson County. The oldest son, John-Boy, kept a journal about his family and yearned to be a writer. He began by establishing his own newspaper. What did he call it?

Q825. Jason, the next son, was seeking musical fame. He attended the Clyneburg Conservatory and played with what band?

Q826. The oldest girl, Mary Ellen, became a nursing student, while sister Erin first worked as a telephone operator. When World War II broke out, where did Erin find work?

Q827. Jim-Bob and Elizabeth were the youngest Waltons. Jim-Bob was a twin and, while not specifically stated, his brother died at birth. Had he survived, what name would he have had?

Q828. Ike Godsey owned the town's general store. The phone had three short and one long ring and Ike had a special hiding place for the store's keys. Where was it?

A821. Par-a-Kee

A822. The Boom Boom Room

The Waltons

A823. Rome Walton

A824. *The Blue Ridge Chronicle*

A825. Bobby Bigelow and His Hayseed Gang

A826. Pickett Metal Products Company

A827. Joseph Zebulon

A828. The coffee grinder

The Waltons continued

Q829. Miss Emily and Miss Mamie were spinster sisters who were friends of the Waltons. Although known bootleggers, they didn't tend to think of themselves as breaking the law. What did they call the moonshine they made?

Q830. The Waltons had a number of pets: a dog, a mule, a cow, a goat, a cat, and a peacock. Give the names of any two.

Q831. Charlottesville was the nearest major city and the White Arrow Bus Lines served the area. What were Jefferson County's neighboring towns?

Wonder Woman
ABC, 1976–79

Q832. Paradise Island, located in the Bermuda Triangle, was ruled by a race of Amazons who lived in peace. These women had incredible strength and the ability to run and jump at an accelerated speed. What was the first commandment of Paradise Island?

Q833. Amazons could find Paradise Island "because we know where it is." What prevented anyone else from finding this uncharted island?

Q834. Amazons wore bracelets made of what metal that can be found only on Paradise Island?

Q835. The bracelets possessed by Amazons were part of the process to help them deflect bullets. What other aspect, found only in an Amazon, could make her attempt "bullets and bracelets"?

Q836. If by chance an uninvited visitor came onto Paradise Island, the Amazons had the ability to erase that person's memory of them and of the island with a special drug. From what tree did this drug come?

A829.   "Papa's Recipe"

A830.   Reckless (dog), Blue (mule), Chance (cow), Myrtle (goat), Calico (cat), Rover (peacock)

A831.   Hickory Creek and Waynesboro

Wonder Woman

A832.   "To never tell anyone about it"

A833.   Refraction of light

A834.   Feminum

A835.   "The Amazon mind is conditioned for athletic ability. Only we have the speed and coordination to attempt this."

A836.   The Hybernia Tree

Kid Shows, Science Fiction Series and Westerns

The Adventures of Superboy
Syndicated, 1988–91

Q837. This series followed the adventures of Clark Kent before he became Superman and moved to Metropolis. For what organization did Clark work here, prior to his job with the *Daily Planet*?

Q838. Before relocating to Florida to take the job mentioned in the above question, Clark attended Schuster University and wrote for the school newspaper. What was it called?

Q839. Like almost everyone, Clark had to get up for work. At what time did his alarm clock ring?

Q840. Kryptonite, of course, is the one menace that can kill Clark. In this series, there was only one known supply of the green substance. Where was it?

The Adventures of Superman
Syndicated, 1953–57

Q841. In the classic opening theme, as the announcer intoned "More powerful than a locomotive," a diesel engine was seen (color episodes). What was the roadname of that engine?

The Adventures of Superboy

A837. The Bureau of Extra Normal Matters

A838. *The Herald*

A839. 6:30 A.M.

A840. The Shift Military Institute

The Adventures of Superman

A841. Southern Pacific

The Adventures of Superman continued

Q842. Clark worked for the *Daily Planet* so he could learn of fast-breaking stories and act quickly as Superman. How much did a copy of the paper cost?

Q843. Prior to becoming the editor of the *Daily Planet*, Perry White held two jobs. What were they?

Q844. Clark lived in a small apartment in Metropolis. What was the name of the hotel and what was his apartment number?

Alien Nation
Fox, 1989–90

Q845. Little Tencton, an area in Los Angeles, was where a group of aliens from the planet Tencton lived. Among them were George Francisco and his wife Susan. What was George's alien name?

Q846. The aliens were referred to as the Newcomers as well as by what slang term?

Q847. In order to reproduce, Newcomers required a husband, a wife, and a special mating alien. What was this special alien called?

Q848. Newcomer women were sexually aroused by what Earth TV public service announcement?

Andy's Gang
NBC, 1955–58

Q849. "I gotta gang, you gotta gang, everybody's gotta have a gang; but there's only one gang for me—good old Andy's Gang." Who could forget that great opening theme to this classic kid's show? Host Andy Devine most often began each episode with "Andy's Story Time." What was the title of that big book he opened before he read a chapter from it?

A842. Five cents

A843. Newspaper reporter, then mayor of Metropolis

A844. The Standish Arms Hotel, Apartment 5H

Alien Nation

A845. Neemo

A846. "Slags"

A847. A Binon

A848. The piercing tone of an emergency broadcast test

Andy's Gang

A849. *Andy's Stories*

Andy's Gang continued

Q850. There was also a regular weekly segment with Midnight the Cat and Squeaky the Mouse. What musical instrument did Squeaky play?

Q851. At the end of the program, before the closing theme, Andy appeared to bid farewell for this Saturday morning and to remind kids not to forget something. What was it?

Annie Oakley
Syndicated, 1954–57

Q852. Annie Oakley, TV's earliest heroine, invariably hit what she aimed at ("Once Annie aims at something it's a bullseye"). In the opening theme, she shot a hole in the center of what playing card?

Q853. Target and later Daisy were Annie's horses. Her brother, Tagg, also had a horse. What was its name?

Q854. Annie had a special area outside of town that she turned into a game preserve (Tagg's rabbit, Mr. Hoppity, lived there). What did Annie call this area?

Astro Boy
Syndicated, 1963

Q855. "Crowds will cheer you, you're a hero, go go Astro Boy." The theme hailed the exploits of the robot Astro Boy as he battled evil. Astro Boy, however, was created under tragic circumstances when a scientist lost his son in a car accident and created the robot in the boy's image. What was the boy's real name?

Q856. "I hearby christen thee my robot son, Astro Boy" was said by the real boy's father, Professor Boynton, when electricity gave the robot life one year later. The robot was taught and learned all there was to know, but it failed to mature. A disgusted Boynton sold the robot to a circus sideshow. Who bought Astro Boy?

A850. The ukulele

A851. Andy's closing speech: "Yes sir, we're pals and pals stick together. And now don't forget church or Sunday school..."

Annie Oakley

A852. Nine of spades

A853. Pixie

A854. Annie's Ark

Astro Boy

A855. Aster Boynton

A856. The Great Catchatori

Astro Boy continued

Q857. When Dr. Elefun discovered what happened he rescued Astro Boy from the circus by having a law passed that freed robots. What was this law called?

Q858. Dr. Elefun had an I.Q. of 138 and headed the Institute of Science. Astro Boy had superhuman strength, super hearing, and rockets in his feet. How much horsepower did the rockets' motors produce to enable Astro Boy to fly?

Battlestar Galactica
ABC, 1978–79

Q859. After their world was destroyed by the evil Cylons, a group of survivors banded together to follow the Galactica, a giant battlestar ship, as it searched for the planet Earth. How many ships were following the Galactica?

Q860. The commander of the Galactica was Adama, who was assisted by his children, Starbuck, Apollo, and Athena. His wife, however, was killed in the final confrontation that destroyed their home planet. What was Adama's wife's name?

Q861. Starbuck's romantic interest was the beautiful Cassiopea. She was a socialator (high-priced call girl) and objected to Starbuck smoking cigars. What did her name mean?

Q862. The Galacticans' enemies were the Cylon warriors. What were these warriors called and what type of ships did they pilot?

Q863. Adama lived on the planet Caprica, one of the twelve home planets that were destroyed. What was the mother planet called?

A857. The Robot Bill of Rights

A858. 100,000

Battlestar Galactica

A859. 220

A860. Lila

A861. "Fairy Queen"

A862. Raiders were the warriors; Vipers were their ships

A863. Cobor

The Beany and Cecil Show
ABC, 1963–67

Q864. Beany, the freckle-faced boy, and Cecil, the seasick sea serpent, assisted Horatio K. Huffenpuff, captain of the *Leakin' Lena*, as they sought adventure. Horatio possessed a trophy for what distinction?

Q865. He was voted villain of the year and he was the captain's enemy, "the do-badder who hates do-gooders." Who was he?

Q866. Cecil called himself "tall, green, and gruesome" and had a favorite TV star. Who was she?

The Big Valley
ABC, 1965–69

Q867. Victoria Barkley and her grown children, Jarrod, Heath, Nick, and Audra, owned the Barkley Ranch in the San Joaquin Valley in Stockton, California. The ranch comprised how many acres?

Q868. On the trail Heath Barkley was famous for what meal?

Q869. Heath's good luck charm was a bit unusual because if it were alive it could kill him. What was it?

Q870. Nick was the ranch foreman and an expert on horses. He was fond of one particular horse that he had had for a long time. What was its name?

Q871. Victoria also had a horse that she rode on a regular basis. What was the name of her horse?

Bonanza
NBC, 1959–73

Q872. Ben Cartwright and sons Adam, Hoss, and Little Joe owned the Ponderosa Ranch in the Comstock Lode Country near Virginia City, Nevada. It was a vast timberland ranch. How many square miles was it?

The Beany and Cecil Show

A864. "World's Greatest Liar"

A865. Dishonest John

A866. Dinah Shore

The Big Valley

A867. 30,000

A868. Bullfrog stew

A869. The rattler from a rattlesnake

A870. Coco

A871. Misty Girl

Bonanza

A872. 1,000

Bonanza *continued*

Q873. Ranch hands were always treated well by the Cartwrights and earned a decent wage. What was their pay?

Q874. Each of the Cartwright sons had a different mother. Adam was by Elizabeth Stoddard, Hoss by Inger Borgstrom, and Little Joe by Marie DeMarne. What was Hoss's first name (Hoss is his middle name and it was Swedish for a big friendly man)?

Q875. Ben rode a horse named Buck. Name Little Joe's and Hoss's horses.

Branded
NBC, 1965–66

Q876. "Branded, marked with a coward's shame. What do you do when you're branded and you know you're a man? Wherever you go for the rest of your life you must prove you're a man. Branded." Jason McCord, an ex-army captain, was branded "the coward of Bitter Creek" for deserting his troops during a Comanche attack. He had been knocked unconscious and woke up in a farmer's house some miles from the scene, unable to explain what happened. But because of Horace Greeley's newspaper columns about Jason's cowardice, Jason was also known by what two other names?

Q877. Jason was born in Washington, D.C., and attended West Point. What soon-to-become-famous general did Jason, a cadet, coach on his entrance exams?

Q878. The skills Jason learned in the army allowed him to establish a company with his grandfather, Gen. Joshua McCord. What did they call the business?

Bronco
ABC, 1958–60

Q879. Bronco Layne was "born down around the old Panhandle" and "there ain't a horse that he can't handle, that's how he got his name." Bronco served with the Texas Confederacy and had a reminder of the Battle of Elmira. What was it?

A873. $30 a month, a bunk, and beans

A874. Eric

A875. Cochise (Little Joe's horse) and Chuck (Hoss's horse)

Branded

A876. "Yellow Tail" and "Yellow Belly"

A877. George Armstrong Custer

A878. McCord & McCord, Survey Engineers

Bronco

A879. A cat he called Elmira

Bronco continued

Q880. Bronco also had a pocket watch that played what particular song when it was opened?

Q881. Inside the pocket watch was a picture of the only girl Bronco ever loved (they grew up in Texas together). Who was she?

Captain Scarlet and the Mysterons
Syndicated, 1967

Q882. Spectrum, a futuristic organization, had been established to safeguard the Earth. Where was Spectrum headquartered?

Q883. The Mysterons were aliens who declared war on Earth when they mistook an exploration of their planet by Spectrum as an unprovoked attack. What planet was Spectrum battling?

Q884. Captain Scarlet was Spectrum's chief operative and Colonel White was the organization's commander-in-chief. Other agents included Lieutenant Green, Captain Blue, and Captain Magenta. What did all Spectrum agents have in common?

Captain Video and His Video Rangers
DuMont, 1949–57

Q885. Captain Video was "The Guardian of the safety of the world." He operated from a secret mountain headquarters and battled Earth's enemies. Dr. Pauli was one of the captain's most diabolical nemeses. What society did Dr. Pauli head?

Q886. Commissioner Bell was the captain's superior. He was based on the 144th floor of what building in Planet City?

A880. "Deep in the Heart of Dixie"

A881. Redemption McNally

Captain Scarlet and the Mysterons

A882. Cloudbase

A883. Mars

A884. They are all named after the colors of the Spectrum.

Captain Video

A885. The Asteroidal Society

A886. The Public Safety Building

Captain Video *continued*

Q887. When the series was broadcast live, action scenes from old theatrical films were shown to allow costume and set changes. The actors in these films were said to be video rangers fighting for justice. What device did Captain Video use to tune into these rangers in the field?

Cheyenne
ABC, 1956–63

Q888. Cheyenne Bodie was the name a twelve-year-old boy, the survivor of an Indian massacre on a wagon train, took when he chose to leave the Cheyenne tribe that raised him. What Indian name did the boy have?

Q889. A wanderer, the grown Cheyenne took whatever jobs he could find. He hoped one day to settle down. What were his plans when the time came?

Q890. Cheyenne was trusted by Indian chiefs and could read smoke signals. On the right side of his holster he carried a gun; what did he have on the left side?

Colt .45
ABC, 1957–60

Q891. Chris Colt was an undercover agent for the government who posed as a salesman for the Colt .45. By what other name was the gun known?

Q892. The gun had a finely milled butt "that seems to jump in the hand." How much did a Colt .45 cost?

Q893. Chris would not sell his demonstrators ("I'd be out of business if I did that"). Once a gun was ordered from Chris how long did it take before it arrived?

A887. The Remote Carrier Delayed Circuit TV Screen

Cheyenne

A888. Grey Fox

A889. Buy a ranch and raise horses

A890. A hunting knife

Colt .45

A891. "The Peacemaker"

A892. $20

A893. Six months

Dr. Quinn, Medicine Woman
CBS, 1993–

Q894. Michaela Quinn is a doctor in Colorado Springs in 1865, distrusted by most of the townspeople (who don't cotton to female doctors). This is no surprise to Michaela, who had a difficult time finding a medical school back east that would admit a woman. What school did Michaela attend?

Q895. The local Cheyenne Indians think Michaela is "a crazy white woman" because "only white men make medicine." Everything changes when she saves the life of the Cheyenne chief. What Indian name does the chief give her?

Dudley Do-Right of the Mounties
ABC, 1969–70

Q896. Dudley Do-Right was a simple-minded Mountie with the Canadian Mounted Police in North Alberta. He was honest to a fault and had been called "the man who can do no wrong." Dudley, however, became a disgrace to the Mounties one night at dinner for doing what despicable deed?

Q897. Sawmill owner Snidley Whiplash was "that meaner than mean, downright villainous, no good villain of the Northwest" who was constantly pursued by Dudley. He also had this uncontrollable urge to do something that could cost Inspector Ray K. Fenwick's daughter, Nell, her life. What was it?

The Eighth Man
Syndicated, 1965

Q898. "Quick call Tobor, the Eighth Man, the mightiest robot of them all" the theme exclaimed when evil threatened the Earth. Mr. Tobor, as he was called, was a private detective who was actually a robot created by Professor Genius. Tobor worked in Metro City and was a police officer before he was "killed" by Saucer Lip. Who was this police officer?

Dr. Quinn, Medicine Woman

A894. The Women's Medical College of Pennsylvania

A895. "Medicine Woman"

Dudley Do-Right of the Mounties

A896. He ate peas with a knife—"something a mountie would never do."

A897. Tying ladies to railroad tracks

The Eighth Man

A898. Peter Brady (Professor Genius embodied Brady's life force into that of the robot)

The Eighth Man *continued*

Q899. Mr. Tobor was head of the Tobor Detective Agency and often worked with the police department. Who was its chief?

Q900. Tobor had to take an energy booster to maintain his strength when he battled evil, such as Intercrime. Based on Intercrime Island, it was a threat to the safety of the world. Its symbol was a dagger plunged into the world. Who was its head?

The Flintstones
ABC, 1960–66

Q901. Fred and Wilma Flintstone and neighbors Betty and Barney Rubble resided in the town of Bedrock in the year 1,000,040 B.C. Fred and Barney toiled at the Slaterock Gravel Company. Before being laid off and finding a job with Fred's company, Barney worked for a rival outfit. What was it?

Q902. Fred and Barney were members of the Bedrock Quarry baseball team and their favorite TV show was *Jay Bondrock*. The two also enjoyed bowling and were members of what lodge?

Q903. Barney and Betty had a pet Hoparoo called Hoppy while Fred and Wilma had a six-foot-tall, purple-with-black-spots pet named Dino. What kind of dinosaur was Dino?

Q904. Fred loved to eat, and although Wilma "fixes the best dodo bird in Bedrock," his favorite meal was something else. Name it.

George of the Jungle
ABC, 1967–70

Q905. In Africa lived George of the Jungle, a mighty hero who didn't know the meaning of the word fear ("But George can look it up"). What province in Africa did George protect?

A899. Chief Fumble Thumbs

A900. Dr. Spectre

The Flintstones

A901. The Pebble Rock and Gravel Company

A902. The Royal Order of the Water Buffalo

A903. Snarkasaurus

A904. Bronto Burgers

George of the Jungle

A905. The Mbweebee Valley

George of the Jungle continued

Q906. Rather naive, George had a problem with trees—he crashed into them when swinging from vine to vine like Tarzan. He had an ape named Ape and a mate called Ursula, as well as what prized possession?

The Ghost Busters
CBS, 1975–76

Q907. Spenser and Kong were ghost busters. They were assisted by a trained gorilla named Tracy and attempted to rid people's lives of ghosts with a ray gun–like weapon. What was it called?

Q908. The trio operated from a rather run-down office building that looked like it was about to be condemned. They took orders from a never-seen superior via a tape recording (as on *Mission Impossible*). Who was their boss?

The Guns of Will Sonnett
ABC, 1967–69

Q909. Jeff Sonnett had never seen his father, James; Jeff's grandfather, Will Sonnett, was determined that the two meet. A trek was begun to find James, a wanted gunman and killer, who deserted his family twenty years earlier (1852) after his wife died while giving birth. Will took on the responsibility of raising Jeff. Where did the Sonnetts live at this time?

Q910. The road Will and Jeff traveled was a difficult one because James was unaware that his kin were seeking him. While James may have been thought of as a killer, he aided people in trouble, and would kill only in self-defense. He carried with him a gold watch that was given to him by Will. What was the inscription in it?

Q911. Will was fast on the draw and James showed promise; "Trouble is, he left before I taught him half what I know." When faced with an opponent, Will would comment, "They say James is fast. Well, he ain't, I am." He ended each statement with what famous four-word catchphrase?

A906. His rhinestone yo-yo

The Ghost Busters

A907. A Ghost Dematerializer

A908. Mr. Zero

The Guns of Will Sonnett

A909. Bensfort, Wyoming

A910. "To James From His Loving Father"

A911. "No brag, just fact"

Have Gun—Will Travel
CBS, 1957–62

Q912. "Have Gun—Will Travel reads the card of a man, a knight without armor in a savage land." The words of the theme told of Paladin, a fast gun for hire who operated out of what hotel in San Francisco?

Q913. Paladin had box seats at the opera house, enjoyed fine food, smoked expensive cigars, and has an eye for the ladies. He also collected chessmen and had one rule. What was it?

Q914. A graduate of West Point, Paladin had a talent with a gun. He often read out-of-state newspapers and sent his calling card to people he felt might need his help. What was his fee?

Hotel de Paree
CBS, 1959–60

Q915. A man known only as Sundance was an ex-gunfighter turned lawman in Georgetown, Colorado in the 1870s. He turned his life around after serving a prison term and was now partners with Annette Devereaux in the Hotel de Paree, a fancy hotel and gambling hall. From what town and state did Sundance hail?

Q916. Also known as the Sundance Kid, he had a gun but would wear it only when necessary. He also sported a black Stetson with a hatband of small, highly polished mirrors that, when the sun shown on them, blinded opponents in gunfights. How many mirrors were on the hatband?

Q917. Sundance carried a Colt .45, had a knack for whittling and a dog who was always by his side. What was the dog's name?

Have Gun—Will Travel

A912. The Carlton

A913. "Never to go anyplace without my gun."

A914. $1,000

Hotel de Paree

A915. Tombstone, Arizona

A916. Ten

A917. Useless

Howdy Doody
NBC, 1947–60

Q918. While Buffalo Bob Smith tried to keep the peace in Doodyville, the nasty Phineas T. Bluster attempted to see that people had no fun. His assistant was Chief Thunderthud. To what Indian tribe did the chief belong?

Q919. Howdy Doody and his brother were born in Doodyville, Texas, on December 27, 1941, to parents who earned a living by performing chores for the ranch owner. What did Mr. and Mrs. Doody name Howdy's brother?

Isis
CBS, 1975–78

Q920. "O Mighty Isis" were the words Andrea Thomas spoke to become Isis, a daring defender of the underdog. Andrea had the power to become Isis by the magic of something she found while on an expedition in Egypt. What was it?

Q921. When Andrea became Isis, she was able to soar and had power over animals and control over the elements of earth, sea, and sky. When not battling evil, she was teaching what subject in high school?

Q922. Rick Mason, Andrea's friend, was a teacher and boating enthusiast who was unaware of her secret alias. What was his boat called?

Jeff's Collie
CBS, 1954–57

Q923. Jeff Miller lived on a farm in Calverton with his widowed mother, Ellen, and grandfather, George, who was affectionately called "Gramps." Jeff's dog, Lassie, was inherited from a neighbor. What was the neighbor's name?

Q924. A volunteer fireman and head of the school board, Gramps was born on the land he owned and on which he raised his family. He also had a term for people who irritated him. What was it?

Howdy Doody

A918. The Ooragnak Tribe (Ooragnak is Kangaroo spelled backwards)

A919. Double Doody

Isis

A920. A magic amulet

A921. Science

A922. *Star Tracker*

Jeff's Collie

A923. Homer Carey

A924. "Pusillanimous Polecat"

Jeff's Collie continued

Q925. Jeff and his friend, Porky Brockway, were blood brothers. Porky had a dog named Pokey, and Porky and Jeff had a special signal for each other. What was it?

Q926. Porky was overweight; his parents were on the hefty side; and Pokey, a basset hound, could have lost some poundage. What was Pokey's official name?

The Jetsons
ABC, 1962–63

Q927. The Jetsons were a twenty-first-century family. George and Jane were the parents, and Judy and Elroy were their children. In what housing complex did the family live?

Q928. George was in the army reserve (U.S. Space Guards Division) and worked for Spacely Space Sprockets. How many sprockets a day did the company produce?

Q929. Fifteen-year-old Judy had a talking diary she called Di Di and attended what school?

Q930. Elroy, her eight-year-old brother, had a dog named Astro and was a member of the Little Dipper League baseball team. What grammar school did he attend?

Johnny Ringo
CBS, 1959–60

Q931. Johnny Ringo was a gunfighter who went on the other side of the law to become sheriff of Velardi, Arizona. Johnny believed that the town hired his guns, not him, because his reputation was known from the Gulf to the Pacific Ocean. How much a month did he earn as sheriff?

Q932. Johnny had an unusual gun, a variation on the French firearm, the Le Met Special. It was designed by his friend, Cason Thomas, "to even up the odds." The gun looked like a regular Colt .45 but it had a separate barrel located under the standard one. What type of bullet did this barrel fire?

A925.   "Eee-ock-eee"

A926.   Pokerman III

The Jetsons

A927.   The Sky Pad Apartments

A928.   Three million

A929.   Orbit High

A930.   The Little Dipper School

Johnny Ringo

A931. $200

A932.   A .410 shotgun shell

Land of the Lost
NBC, 1974–77

Q933. Forest ranger Rick Marshall and his children, Will and Holly, were rafting down the Colorado River when they were caught in a time vortex and transported to a land of prehistoric creatures. When the Marshalls found they could not escape, they established a home in a cave. What did they call their home?

Q934. Strange pyramid-like triangles controlled this alien land, and inside them were colored crystals that could open a time doorway to freedom if the right sequence could be found. What were these triangles called?

Lawman
ABC, 1958–62

Q935. "The Lawman came with the sun; there was a job to be done; so they sent for the badge and the gun of the Lawman." The man is Dan Troop, the marshal of Laramie, Wyoming, a town that "is tough on lawmen and horse thieves." When living back in Texas, Dan was the marshal of Abilene and became a legend. What was he called?

Q936. The Birdcage Saloon was the town's watering hole and the Blue Bonnet Cafe was the eatery. What was the name of the local newspaper?

Lost in Space
CBS, 1965–68

Q937. An attempt to explore a new planet failed when the space ship was thrown off course and stranded its crew and passengers. Donald West was the ship's pilot and the Robinson family (John, Maureen, and children Judy, Will, and Penny) were on board. Also there was Zachary Smith, an agent who sabotaged the ship. John was a professor of astrophysics and Maureen was a biochemist who was the first woman in U.S. history to do something. What was it?

Land of the Lost

A933. High Bluff

A934. Pylons

Lawman

A935. "The Fast Gun From Texas"

A936. *The Laramie Weekly* or *The Laramie Free Press* (as seen in the pilot)

Lost in Space

A937. Pass the International Space Administration's grueling, emotionally draining test for intergalatic flight

Lost in Space continued

Q938. Penny, with an I.Q. of 147, was interested in zoology; Will held the highest average in the history of his school; and Judy had high hopes of doing something. For what did she "heroically postpone all hopes"?

Q939. Donald West "rocketed the scientific world with his theory of other planets' fitness for human habitation." From what school did he graduate?

Q940. "Bucket of Bolts" and "Pot-bellied pumpkin" were two of the "terms of endearment" Col. Zachary Smith used for the ship's environmental control robot. Smith saw the robot as a slave and had what regular nickname for it?

Q941. The Robot did object to Smith's demands and told him "My computer is not programmed for day and night work. I need eight hours rest like other robots." How did the Robot defend itself?

Maverick
ABC, 1957–62

Q942. "Who is the tall dark stranger there, Maverick is the name..." for brothers Bart and Bret, just this side of honorable gentlemen gamblers who roamed the Old West in search of rich prey. Their daddy, Beauregard "Pappy" Maverick, left each of his sons two things: profound words of wisdom ("Never hold a kicker and never draw to an inside straight") and what else?

Q943. It was against a Maverick's principle to drink alone and the boys had one serious vice. What was it?

Q944. Cousin Beau was the "white sheep" of the family, bringing honor to the Maverick name when he was credited with capturing a Union general during the Civil War. He also rode a horse with a rather unusual name. What was it?

A938. "A career in the musical comedy field"

A939. The Center for Radio Astronomy

A940. "Booby"

A941. With electrical discharges

Maverick

A942. A $1,000 bill

A943. Curiosity

A944. Gumlegs

The Marvel Super Heroes
Syndicated, 1965

Q945. "The Incredible Hulk," "Iron Man," "Captain America," "Sub Mariner," and "The Mighty Thor" were adapted to TV in animated form on this series. Donald Blake was the secret identity of the Mighty Thor, who had superhuman strength and the abilities of a Norse God. He also had a virtually indestructible throwing weapon. What was it called?

Q946. "When Captain America throws his mighty shield, all those who chose to oppose his shield must yield; and the red, the white, and the blue will come true when Captain America throws his mighty shield." Captain America, who stood six feet two and weighed 240 pounds, posed as an army private. He had abilities in speed and strength and his weapon was his shield. What name did he use as a cover?

Q947. Industrialist Tony Stark was secretly Iron Man. He wore an electronically powered suit of armor which increased his strength to superhuman levels. With the armor he stood six feet four inches tall. How much did he weigh?

The Mickey Mouse Club
ABC, 1955–59

Q948. "Who's the leader of the club that's made for you and me?" The opening line of the theme meant it was time for a daily visit with the Mouseketeers. Jimmie Dodd led the festivities, and each weekday was devoted to a specific subject (for example, Monday was "Fun With Music Day"). Name the other four days' shows.

Q949. "Time to twist our Mousekedial to the right and the left with a great big smile. This is the way we get to see a Mouse Cartoon for you and me." Finish the line that would open the Mickey Mouse Treasure Mine.

The Marvel Super Heroes

A945. Mjolnir, his enchanted hammer

A946. Steve Rogers

A947. 640 pounds

The Mickey Mouse Club

A948. Tuesday was Guest Star Day; Wednesday was Anything Can Happen Day; Thursday was Circus Day; Friday was Talent Roundup Day

A949. "Meeska, Mooseka, Mouseketeer, Mouse Cartoon Time Now Is Here."

The Monroes
ABC, 1966–67

Q950. Clayt, Kathleen, Amy, and twins Jefferson and Fennimore Monroe were orphaned children who settled in "Pa's Valley," a patch of wilderness in Wyoming to which their father, Albert, laid claim in 1866. What item of Albert's marked the claim?

Q951. While the Monroes called it "Pa's Valley," ranchers Barney Wales and Major Mapoy called it by its actual name. What is the official name of the valley?

National Velvet
NBC, 1960–62

Q952. Twelve-year-old Velvet Brown dreamed of owning a horse and training it for the Grand National Steeplechase. Part of her dream came true when she won a beautiful chestnut thoroughbred in a raffle. While Velvet (and everyone else) called the horse King, that was not his full name. What was it?

Q953. Velvet won several local competitions with King, including the Junior Hurdles. The horse was not hard to train, but Velvet did have one serious problem. What was it?

Q954. The Brown family owned a dairy farm in an area called the Valley. They sold their milk in neighboring Flintwood at what dairies?

Pistols 'n' Petticoats
CBS, 1966–67

Q955. Wretched, Colorado, was a wild and woolly town with a sheriff, Harold Sykes, but it was the Hanks family who maintained the law and order. Harold has instituted an antilittering ordinance called "Wretched Beautiful." How much was the fine for breaking the law?

The Monroes

A950. His army belt buckle

A951. Bear Valley

National Velvet

A952. Blaze King

A953. Breaking him to saddle

A954. The Winters Dairies

Pistols 'n' Petticoats

A955. Fifty cents

Pistols 'n' Petticoats continued

Q956. Henrietta Hanks was a widow with a daughter named Lucy, and lived on a ranch with Henrietta's mother and father. Henrietta "could fire a gun with one hand milking a goat and hit a coyote on the run." Andrew, her father, "kept his gun in trim; nobody messed around with him," and had a mule and a pet wolf. The mule was Molly, but what was the wolf named?

Planet of the Apes
CBS, 1974

Q957. Pete Burke and Alan Virdon were the U.S. astronauts marooned on a planet of highly intelligent apes in this TV adaptation of the feature films. Here Pete and Alan had crashlanded in an area that was previously called California. What had the ape leaders renamed it?

Q958. Alan and Pete believe that the only way to return to their time was by reversing the ship's magnetic disc, which recorded the flight. They had two problems with this theory. One was finding a computer; what was the other?

Punky Brewster
NBC/Syndicated, 1984–88

Q959. Punky Brewster was a seven-year-old girl, abandoned by her parents but adopted by a gruff photographer named Henry Warnimont. Although called "Gunky" Brewster at school, this adorable little girl had a real first name. What was it?

Q960. "That's Punky Power!" was one of Punky's catchphrases. What was "Punky Power"?

Q961. Margaux Kramer, Punky's very rich and spoiled girlfriend, took lessons from her mother on how to fire servants. She felt that the closest she would ever come to poverty was when she visited Punky at home. Margaux had a collection of dolls and one in particular was her favorite, a dancing ballerina that played what song that comforted her when she was sad?

A956. Bowzer

Planet of the Apes

A957. Central City

A958. A human intelligent enough to build a ship

Punky Brewster

A959. Penelope

A960. "No matter how bad things look, everything will be all right."

A961. "Beautiful Dreamer"

Quantum Leap
NBC, 1989–93

Q962. Dr. Samuel Beckett created Quantum Leap as a means of traveling through time. It was a top secret government project and was hidden in the New Mexico desert thirty miles from what town?

Q963. A system malfunction had trapped Sam in time and he could travel only within thirty years of his own lifetime. In his "leaps," Sam assumed the identities of people he had never known, to correct a mistake in their lives. Where did these people bide their time while Sam was assuming their identity?

Q964. Al Calavicci was a project observer whose holographic image appeared to Sam through brainwave transmissions. Sam was the only person who was supposed to see Al, but this was not so. Who else could see Al?

Q965. Sam had a specific reason for creating Quantum Leap and spent over a billion dollars developing it. What was the reason?

Quark
NBC, 1978

Q966. Betty I and Betty II were the copilots of a galaxy scow piloted by Adam Quark. Betty II was a clone of Betty I. Where was the cell taken from Betty I to create Betty II?

Q967. The ship Adam piloted patrolled the deep regions of space picking up the trash of other planets in the United Galaxies. How much compacted trash could Adam's ship hold?

Rango
ABC, 1967

Q968. "I'm Rango, just Rango, Texas Ranger" said Rango when asked his name. He was dimwitted, slow on the draw, and a major headache to his captain. In what Texas Ranger outpost was Rango stationed?

Quantum Leap

A962. Destiny County

A963. The Waiting Room at the Quantum Leap complex

A964. Dogs, certain children, and mentally unstable people

A965. "To make the world a better place and to make right what was once wrong."

Quark

A966. Under her fingernail

A967. 200,000 pounds

Rango

A968. Gopher Gulch

Rango continued

Q969. Rango believed that a law-abiding town is a happy town and had made eighty-four proclamations. Number one was "No guns allowed in town." What was number 84?

Rocky and His Friends
ABC, 1959–61

Q970. Twenty-nine people resided in Frostbite Falls, Minnesota. Two of them were Rocky the Flying Squirrel and his dimwitted friend, Bullwinkle the Moose. The town was serviced by the Union Pathetic Railroad and had only one movie theater, the Bijou. What was the first film shown at the theater?

Q971. Each year Rocky and Bullwinkle vacationed on "the wettest, soggiest, dreariest place on earth." What was this location?

Q972. Rocky was the all-American squirrel and wore an aviator's cap. He also said what (his catchphrase) when something went wrong?

Q973. It was difficult for Bullwinkle to follow the story and be part of it at the same time, and he relied on the show's narrator to help him. Through this narration Bullwinkle learned that his uncle discovered something that was now his claim to fame. What was it?

Q974. Dastardly Boris Badanov was "the world's lowest snake in the grass." He and his villainous assistant, Natasha, worked for Mr. Big (a midget who casts a giant shadow) and operated from where?

Saved by the Bell
NBC, 1989–

Q975. Kelly, Jesse, Lisa, Zack, Screech, and Slater are the featured students at Bayside High School in what fictional town in California?

A969.   "No whistling at girls on the street"

Rocky and His Friends

A970.   *A Trolley Named Tallulah*

A971.   An island called Moosylvania

A972.   "Hoakie Smokes"

A973.   A metal called Upsadaisium

A974.   The Old Bleakley House

Saved by the Bell

A975.   Palisades

Saved by the Bell continued

Q976. The Max is the after-school hangout and Kelly worked there as a waitress. Kelly knows she is very beautiful but fears someone will discover she is not perfect. What does she dread someone will learn about her?

Q977. Lisa loves shopping ("Lisa is my name and shopping is my game") and claims she has an ability no one else has. What is it?

Q978. Zack is the rich preppy student who became Principal Richard Belding's "Zack Ache" for all the aggravation he has caused with his pranks. One was a chance to make money by issuing the Girls of Bayside High Swimsuit Calendar. Kelly, Jesse, and Lisa were featured as month girls. Name the months each was a "Miss."

Q979. Screech was a fifth runner-up in an ALF lookalike contest and has a robot named Kevin as well as a dog, roach, mouse, lizard, spider, and two rats. Give the names for any two of these pets.

Sheena, Queen of the Jungle
Syndicated, 1956–57

Q980. Sheena was a female version of Tarzan, and the show featured Irish McCalla as the shapely blond jungle goddess. Like Tarzan, Sheena had a simian companion. What was his name?

Q981. And, like Tarzan, who had Jane, Sheena had a male friend, a white trader who assisted her. Name him.

Space 1999
Syndicated, 1975–77

Q982. It was the year 1999 and the moon had been blasted out of its orbit. Moonbase, as it was called, was now home to the 311 men and women assigned to it. John Koenig was the commander and Dr. Helena Russell the chief medical officer. As the moon drifted in space, the Earthlings encountered life forms from other planets. What did aliens call the residents of Moonbase Alpha?

A976.   She wears a retainer at night.

A977.   To guess the contents of a gift package without opening it.

A978.   Kelly was "Miss November"; Jesse "Miss July"; Lisa "Miss October"

A979.   Hound Dog (dog), Herbert (roach), Arnold (mouse), Oscar (lizard), Ted (spider)

Sheena, Queen of the Jungle

A980.   Chim

A981.   Bob Rayburn

Space 1999

A982.   Alphans

Space 1999 continued

Q983. Maya was an alien who became a member of Moonbase Alpha in second-season episodes. She was a metamorph, able to assume any form. From what planet did Maya come?

Space Rangers
CBS, 1993

Q984. In the year 2104 a renegade band of Space Rangers battles evil throughout the universe. John Boon is the captain and his crew includes Doc, Jo Jo, and Zylyn. Doc is the ship's repairman and has seven synthetic body parts. What do Boon and Jo Jo call him?

Q985. They don't tell us what a Zulu is, but it is the favorite drink of the Space Rangers. Where do they like taking their liquid refreshment?

Q986. The Space Rangers are fearless and will battle any enemy that poses a threat to Earth. They live and die by their motto. What is it?

Q987. Jo Jo and Zylyn are both aliens who assist Boon. Zylyn is a master at Zylyusian Flute Sword (like Earth dueling) and Jo Jo is a tall, blond bombshell from a planet where men are wimps. From what planets are Zylyn and Jo Jo?

Sugarfoot
ABC, 1957–60

Q988. A cowboy one grade lower than a tenderfoot was called a sugarfoot. Tom Brewster, a sugarfoot looked upon as a gullible greenhorn by the local roughnecks, was hoping to become a lawyer. All he wanted to do was study his law books. What law book does Tom carry with him?

Q989. Tom felt that guns were "tools of the devil" and that "shootin' ain't always the answer." He was also opposed to alcohol, but did frequent saloons. What drink did he always order?

A983. Psychon

Space Rangers

A984. "Tin Man"

A985. Geno's Bar.

A986. "Into the Jaws of Hell for Justice"

A987. Zylyn is from Grakka; Jo Jo from New Venus

Sugarfoot

A988. *Blackstone's Commentary,* vol. 9

A989. "Sarsaparilla with a touch of cherry"

Time Trax
Syndicated, 1993–

Q990. Darien Lambert is a cop from the future (born on August 17, 2160) who has been sent back in time to 1993 to capture criminals who escape from their futures to our past. With what futuristic organization is Darien associated?

Q991. Police officers of the future, such as Darien, still use guns, but they are not types that kill; they immobilize suspects. What are these guns called?

Q992. Darien is assisted by SELMA, a holographic image that can give him any information that he requires. What does SELMA stand for?

Walker, Texas Ranger
CBS, 1993–

Q993. Cardell Walker is a Texas Ranger with the Department of Public Safety. Although he invariably exceeds his authority, his superiors admit that he is good. What is the name of Walker's horse?

Q994. Alexandra "Alex" Cahill is the prosecuting attorney and believes there is a special place in heaven for Walker. She helps him "so cases will not fall through the cracks of the legal system." Name her horse.

Yancy Derringer
CBS, 1958–59

Q995. Yancy Derringer, a former Confederate soldier, worked undercover for John Colton to help end the rising tide of crime, and was assisted by Pahoo, a nonspeaking Indian. What weapon did Pahoo carry with him at all times?

Q996. Yancy was born on a plantation in Louisiana and owned a riverboat. Name both the plantation and the riverboat.

Q997. He also had a dog and dressed in fancy "duds." Name the dog and the store at which Yancy bought his clothes.

Time Trax

A990. The Fugitive Retrieval System

A991. The Pellet Projection Tube

A992. Specified Encapsulated Limited Memory Archive

Walker, Texas Ranger

A993. Cookie

A994. Amber

Yancy Derringer

A995. A shotgun

A996. Waverly Plantation; the *Sultana*

A997. Old Dixie; Devereaux's Gentleman's Apparel

Zorro

ABC, 1957–59

Q998. Zorro, alias Don Diego, was the mysterious defender of the oppressed in Old Los Angeles. What old proverb prompted Don Diego to adopt the guise of Zorro (the Fox)?

Q999. Zorro was famous for carving his trademark Z. On what object did Zorro put his first Z?

Q1000. Sergeant Garcia was the overweight and bumbling assistant to the evil Captain Monasterio of the King's Lancers. Name Garcia's favorite watering hole.

Bonus

Q1001. Match the characters with the TV or radio stations on which they worked. Also supply the name of the show and the city or town in which it was set.

1. Bailey Quarters	(A) WKS-TV
2. Frasier Crane	(B) WJM-TV
3. Bobby Soul	(C) AFVN-TV
4. Steven Keaton	(D) KBHR (radio)
5. Matt Cassidy	(E) KGGY-TV
6. Jessica Novak	(F) KXLA-TV
7. Gordie Howard	(G) TAB-TV
8. Ellen Cunningham	(H) KACL (radio)
9. Christine Armstrong	(I) WYN-TV
10. Candi LeRoy	(J) WBN-TV
11. Bill Bittinger	(K) KLA-TV
12. Barth Gimble	(L) WKRP (radio)
13. George Owens	(M) UBS-TV
14. Chris Owens	(N) WBLZ (radio)
15. Tabitha Stephens	(O) WBFL-TV

Zorro

A998. "When you cannot clothe yourself in the skin of a lion put on that of a fox."

A999. A page of sheet music on his father's piano

A1000. The Pasada de Los Angeles

Bonus

A1001. 1 and L ("WKRP in Cincinnati")
2 and H ("Frasier"; Seattle)
3 and N ("Rhythm and Blues"; Detroit)
4 and A ("Family Ties"; Ohio)
5 and I ("Goodnight, Beantown"; Boston)
6 and K ("Jessica Novak"; Los Angeles)
7 and B ("The Mary Tyler Moore Show"; Minneapolis)
8 and G ("W.E.B." New York City)
9 and E ("Coach"; Minneapolis)
10 and C ("The Six O'Clock Follies"; Vietnam)
11 and O ("Buffalo Bill"; Buffalo, N.Y.)
12 and M ("America 2-Night"; Alta Coma, California)
13 and J ("Mr. Belvedere"; Pittsburgh)
14 and D ("Northern Exposure"; Cicely, Alaska)
15 and F ("Tabitha"; Los Angeles)